The POWER
of FORGIVENESS

The POWER
of FORGIVENESS

Kenneth Briggs

Based on a film by Martin Doblmeier

Fortress Press
Minneapolis

THE POWER OF FORGIVENESS
Based on a film by Martin Doblmeier

Copyright © 2008 Fortress Press, an imprint of Augsburg Fortress. All rights reserved. Except for brief quotations in critical articles or reviews, no part of this book may be reproduced in any manner without prior written permission from the publisher. Visit http://www.augsburgfortress.org/copyrights/ or write to Permissions, Augsburg Fortress, Box 1209, Minneapolis MN 55440.

Cover images: Amish women walking copyright © Blair Seitz. Used by permission. Bob Enright at Ardoyne Mural and Greeting Session with Mme. Sadr copyright © Journey Films. Used by permission.

All interior images—except for Amish women walking (p. 58) and Elie Wiesel addressing the Bundestag (p. 29)—reproduced courtesy of Journey Films; copyright © Journey Films. Amish women walking courtesy of Blair Seitz; copyright © Blair Seitz. Elie Wiesel photo copyright © Parlamentsarchiv, Deutscher Bundestag. Used by permission.

Cover and book design: Christy J. P. Barker

Library of Congress Cataloging-in-Publication Data

Briggs, Kenneth A.
  The power of forgiveness / Kenneth Briggs.
    p. cm.
  Includes bibliographical references and index.
  ISBN 978–0–8006–6225–7 (alk. paper)
  1. Forgiveness—Religious aspects. I. Title.
  BL65.F67B75 2008
  205'.699—dc22   2008000085

The paper used in this publication meets the minimum requirements of American National Standard for Information Sciences—Permanence of Paper for Printed Library Materials, ANSI Z329.48.1984.

Printed in Canada
12   11   10   09   08   —TC—   2   3   4   5   6   7   8

Contents

Preface

Martin Doblmeier's instinct that the time was ripe for a broad, serious exploration of forgiveness has been proven even more prescient in the nearly four years since he conceived *The Power of Forgiveness*, the film for which this volume serves as a companion. Our time, these earliest years of a new millennium, seems best defined as the age of alienation. The affairs of nations are in suspicious disarray, poisoned by age-old hostilities and current frenzies over terrorism that have driven us as Americans into deeper and deeper levels of fear and defensiveness. As George Orwell might have put it, "security" has come to mean its very opposite, as the feverish pursuit of "peace" has spurred deepening divisions and distrust. Both national and personal bridges are burning at a frightful pace.

There is a better way, yet it takes trust and determination to let go of resentments and anger and stereotypes. It requires a spirit that can alter and end the cycles of revenge. Forgiveness has been a staple of religions and philosophies forever; now the voice of social science is corroborating its teachings by showing in concrete, empirical ways how forgiveness contributes to health and serves as an antidote to alienation.

Given the hardness of human nature, forgiveness can never have been easy. At the same time, it has certainly never been needed more as the stakes for refusing to forgive mount higher.

This book emerged from a meeting of minds between Martin Doblmeier and Michael West. Doblmeier, founder of Journey Films, saw the need for a film on forgiveness and, with his prodigious energies and talents, produced *The Power of Forgiveness* in conjunction with his talented colleagues Dan Juday and Adele Schmidt. While the film was in its final stages, Doblmeier spoke with West, the editor in chief of Fortress Press, about the possibility of publishing a book on the same subject that would relate to the film but be independent of it. The collaboration took root, and plans for the book shaped up. Both men have been invaluable in its development, though neither bears any responsibility for faults that may appear to readers in its contents.

Michael West offered unstinting encouragement and help in completing this book in a short time. Martin Doblmeier, a true, accomplished, professional filmmaker, graciously provided extensive materials from the film's production for use in the book, including images and interviews that we have excerpted at the ends of some chapters.

Writing this book would have been utterly impossible without the gifts and energies of my son, Matthew. It was my great good fortune that he was available for me to employ as a researcher, principal sounding board, and general appraiser of the chapters as they rolled out. Again, the disclaimer: whatever flies might have ended up in the ointment should not be ascribed to him. I am grateful beyond measure.

The POWER *of* FORGIVENESS

Elusive Forgiveness

The Bible begins with a grudge. Adam and Eve irk God. As the original couple, they receive full privileges of the Garden of Eden, carefree: no mortgage hanging over their heads, no need for a retirement plan, no career worries. They have it all so long as they obey God's one tiny little rule against sampling fruit from the tree of knowledge of good and evil. Like every other human being who has ever existed, however, they can't resist testing the system, and help themselves. Hence the grudge.

A miffed God metes out punishment. From then on, there will be no free lunch. Everyone will have to work for a living, childbirth will be painful, they will know shame rather than innocence and face death instead of eternal life. Adam tries to blame Eve, but for whatever reason, neither apologizes to God. They receive their comeuppance and make no effort to patch things up.

Jews and Christians have different answers to the question of how long it took God to get over the violation. In Jewish tradition, God floods the world, promises Noah never to do it again and, further, sends Moses with a with a bevy of guidelines to righteous living, divine laws that afford the Hebrew people an opportunity to win back God's favor. On Mount Sinai, Moses receives the Ten Commandments, which betoken a renewal of the special relationship between God and the people. Through the remainder of the Hebrew Bible, God frequently agonizes over failures of the people to keep the law but never disowns them or imposes further limitations on their basic nature. God's presence, love, mercy, and justice are available through the keeping of the agreement to abide by God's will.

Christians, by comparison, look to the New Testament for resolution. The harmony that was shattered in the Garden of Eden is restored in the life, death, and resurrection of Jesus. The theology of the four Gospels and the letters of St. Paul and others portray Jesus as God in human form, whose mission is to reunite what the original rebelliousness has broken. Paul specifically refers to Jesus as the second Adam who makes up for the errors of the first. Sins are now forgiven, say the Christians, because God's son, Jesus, has both paid the ultimate price by dying at the hands of that sinfulness and overcome the prison of death by rising from the grave.

The mythic drama and tragedy of Eden provide a backdrop for the awareness of our needs to be forgiven and to consider granting forgiveness to others. Our daily lives are suffused, consciously or unconsciously, with a sense of remorse and grudges we hold against others. In Eden-like fashion, we go against our better nature and, in response, try to reckon what to do about it. We can make excuses or duck the truth about ourselves or others, but the irritating, nagging burr usually remains under our saddle. Where do we find

> In Eden-like fashion, we go against our better nature and, in response, try to reckon what to do about it.

relief? When we are enraged by something done against us, logic would appear to dictate a counter-attack at least as harsh. By the same token, it seems reasonable to beg mercy when we are the guilty ones, because we naturally don't like to be punished, and we are likely to think that we were acting under special circumstances that warrant leniency.

This is a book about the complex patterns that emerge from the subject of forgiveness. The assumption behind forgiveness is that the state of guilt and anger that arises from our actions or the actions of others—and the ingrained drive to do something about it—is part of our nature as human beings rather than something we choose to consider. It is part of the warp and woof of daily existence and a standard theme of the world's great religions. Though the setting for this discussion is largely the Western communities of Christianity and Judaism, the wisdom of Buddhism, Hinduism, and Islam plead as ardently for forgiveness in their own right and will receive attention further on.

For most of us, the question of how to discharge this store of psychic energy driving us to distraction makes an enormous difference in how we live. At one time or other, most of us will be caught in the throes of a payback maelstrom. The response may be to react in kind. The masochistic response may be to accuse oneself instead of pointing at the actual wrongdoer. Self-haters inflict wounds on themselves for what they did not do while the self-worshipers heap scorn on everyone but themselves.

Another possibility underlies this book and Martin Doblmeier's probing film, *The Power of Forgiveness*. That option is forgiveness in all of its mystery, all of its elusiveness, all of its fascination. This is the way that suggests breaking the pattern of protective action-reaction flowing from basic survival instincts. It offers a counterintuitive means of handling the restlessness, hurt, and terror. As the film suggests, this option may be powerful, but it isn't self-evidently so. Our own personal lives and the flood of world news reports make it clear that forgiveness is much more the exception than the rule. Forgiveness doesn't correspond to the solution that nations and individuals believe necessary in order to protect their safety, dignity, or honor. It follows, therefore, that those who practice the politics of forgiveness, such as pacifists and nonviolent resisters, are commonly treated as naïve innocents who would allow evil to triumph. Payback rules; forgiveness appears as a strange pause in the midst of warring madness, like that mythic episode from World War I —the bloodiest tit-for-tat war in history—in which troops on both sides fell into momentary peace and quiet before resuming the fight.

Though it might be underutilized, the forgiveness option remains viable, even hopeful, as the Doblmeier film makes clear, because it holds a power whose fuller potential remains untapped. Whatever the real ability of forgiveness to change things for the better, however, neither the film nor wider observation implies that the spirit of our age is attuned to forgiving attitudes. To the contrary, we are in a "security" mode, on heightened alert to strike our enemies in order to safeguard our heritage. Forgiveness is a stranger to those whose villains sit on death row. Nor does the vast majority of Americans appear willing to seek absolution for leaving millions of children behind in underresourced schools and without healthcare. Moreover, as a nation, we remain steadfastly opposed to seeking pardon from any of the alleged victims of our foreign policy in Asia, the Middle East, or Latin America. It simply isn't deemed the way to go.

The possibility that's been highlighted in the Bible and in other religious traditions is, therefore, an embarrassing oddball in our midst, an alternative for the weak but not for the inhabitants of the world's mightiest nation, whose "power" is spoken about as might.

Those who seek this largely hidden alternative do so on the faith that it may not be popular or understood but that it rests on spiritual resources that must be sought, can be found, and bring joy and greater wholeness.

The first chapter of this book delves into a religious understanding of forgiveness that depends finally on otherworldly strength rather than personal, inner resources. The dynamic element in Western religious tradition is obedience to lessons imparted to believers. Christians, for example, are told to forgive because God has already forgiven them. In addition, Jesus raises havoc by saying there is no limit on how many times forgiveness must be practiced and mentions no exceptions. Then he forgives those who crucify him.

Mohandas K. Gandhi, Martin Luther King Jr., Thich Nhat Hanh, and others have echoed the call to forgive in their movements of nonviolent protest and civil disobedience, which are fundamentally rooted in forgiveness and a "higher conscience" or mind.

Religious tradition no longer has a lock on this discussion. Social science has been producing its own proof that forgiveness has far-reaching benefits. Though striking back may seem "normal" to a broad cross-section of society, and may be biologically hard-wired into our brains, researchers are also discovering that letting go of anger and resentment in the process of forgiving others is associated with physical and psychological advantages. The research has been spurred in part by alarm over the prevalence of vengeance-based violence and the search for its causes.

For a society as focused on personal wellness as ours, the effects of forgiveness on health could loom large. For that reason, the second chapter considers the scientific findings and some of their implications. What might there be that helps the tortured spirit? Does this overlap make "forgiveness studies" less religiously or scientifically valid, and would it matter?

When is forgiveness impossible? Chapter three explores the refusal to forgive and the reasons for it. Some wounds are so deep that even though resolving the anger and suffering may be desirable, practically or religiously the aggrieved person may be unable to take the initiative.

In chapter four we take the measure of forgiveness and probe its potential for transforming mired situations in personal, social, and even political realms. Then in chapter five we zero in on the stubborn challenge of one's own failings and the road to self-forgiveness.

The relationship between justice and forgiveness occupies the next chapter, six. Can a people forgive an oppressor without admission of guilt by the oppressor? On a personal level, how does the demand for confession or contrition either facilitate or compromise the granting of forgiveness?

Chapter seven explores the common but neglected situation in which not one but many parties bear some guilt and blame, and require mutual forgiveness.

A final chapter explores forgiveness as indispensable to the survival of a nation. Societies such as Northern Ireland, South Africa, and Lebanon show how difficult it is to obtain even small degrees of forgiveness but how crucial the process is to the functioning of a society.

Forgiveness, then, is available as a tool, a blessing, a process of conversion that can be brought into play when the powder kegs of hatred and revenge are lit. It is a choice that is not much used; yet, from the testimony and the evidence, it holds enormous riches for our bodies, minds, and souls. It is the path seldom taken that actually leads to a better place, if its practitioners are to be believed. How we get there and how we prepare for it remain for discussion in the following pages.

One

Religion

The Amish made it look simple. Ten of their precious little girls had been shot by a madman who had stormed into their peaceful school in Nickel Mines, Pennsylvania, on an October day in 2006. Five had died; five lay wounded. As television crews rushed to the scene with their disaster faces and high-noon voices, the stricken Amish gathered quietly. By spirit and habit, they were not conditioned to respond with outraged cries against the heavens or attacks on the evils of society, as others had done before the cameras in other scenes of tragedy and loss that the media had monitored. No, the Amish enfolded their grief within their normal circle of prayer and daily communion. They didn't speak out. They looked within. They did it together.

Then they took a step that astonished many onlookers in Lancaster County, where they lived, and throughout the wider world. They went to the home of the man who had killed and wounded their children to speak words of forgiveness to the man's family. They did it apparently without a fuss or theological debate or a long process of getting ready. As shown in *The Power of Forgiveness*, they just up and went, because that is what you do to keep your end of the bargain with God and your fellow humans.

CURIOSITY SURROUNDS AN EXTRAORDINARY RELIGIOUS "HABIT"

Donald Kraybill, a scholar and friend of the Amish, explains in the film that forgiveness is for these pious people so inculcated that it has become a spiritual reflex. Children learn it by watching their parents and neighbors forgive and by looking to the example of Jesus—how he acted in the face of injustice or cruelty and

The Amish made it look simple . . .

what he had to say about them. The pattern is a vestige of old forms of "total" community, where learning takes place largely through osmosis. But children in Amish communities also face a surrounding society that offers them many alternatives. Their choice to embrace the Amish tradition is therefore unlike the more insular, stable communities of long ago where absorption into the communal consciousness was automatic. The Amish have to a much larger degree decided to adopt that tradition out of the many options available to them.

Some of the scholars who have begun to study forgiveness weren't sure the Amish behavior was entirely what it appeared to be. Their studies led them to think the forgiveness had come perhaps too easily and prematurely, though they praised the Amish for going a long way toward setting a Christian example. Fred Luskin, the director of the Forgiveness Project at Stanford University and a subject in Doblmeier's film, told the *Deseret Morning News* a few days after the tragedy that he saw the Amish behavior as "laudatory" but questioned the "inner quality of that forgiveness" that came so quickly. "I don't know how you can do that without feeling some of the pain and struggling with your own loss and woundedness." Their devotion to mercy and peace had inclined them

to react to the assault as if it were "a game of Monopoly" whereby God "set the rules," and their duty was "to be kind," Luskin said. Their visit to the murderer's family displayed that extraordinary religious commitment, he added, while those who favored vengeance or justice were examples of "the value and power of our secular conditioning."

Such relatively mild skepticism generally suggested that the Amish might have felt the pressure of their religious convictions to bestow forgiveness before they had adequately "processed" the pain, anger, and grief. The forgiveness scholars had been staking their credibility on their ability to chart a predictable course of how forgiveness works. Some believed the Amish skipped a few stages at their peril, heading straight to the finish line without running the whole race, leaving them vulnerable to the vagaries of untreated hurts and angers later on. Beyond that qualm, the scientists raised the valid and vexing issue of sincerity. It was possible, just possible, that the Amish were going through ritualistic motions by seeking out the murderer's family without really meaning it. Nobody knows the heart of another, of course, and we can be fooled.

Did the Amish cheat a process verified by science? Did the togetherness and mutual support they received reduce or remove their anger and pain? That would defy human experience. Faith may be capable of moving mountains, but even such a faith reinforced by a community of fellow believers cannot free anyone from the common denominator of human agony in losing a child. The pain in its own mortal way is a measure of the love. The sufferings of the "plain people," as they are known, cannot be different from that of the rest of us.

If they weren't spared the anguish, whatever would allow them to fast-track forgiveness? By deduction, the reason would have to lie in the choice of solutions to the despair, a summoning of consolation with the quality of strength that, as Jesus says of divine peace, the "world can neither give nor take away" and rarely seems to comprehend. The consolation of which the Amish and others speak is, to the common mind, amazing yet alien, an endearing but quaint testimony to the power and healing of God that appears to restore the afflicted beyond the categories of scientific comprehension. For the Amish, it expresses itself as a confidence that is not once-for-all, but

> If they weren't spared the anguish, whatever would allow them to fast-track forgiveness?

must be sustained daily. It is not merely an emergency call for help. The Amish go to the home of the killer to offer the comfort of forgiveness with the faith that they have already been showered with divine comfort. Their errand of mercy is predictable, perhaps, but not automatic. Like all other aspects of faith, they say, forgiveness requires daily practice, a repeated renewal of trust and struggle with doubt. They are set apart from much of the world, but they are subject to the very same struggles as their brothers and sisters everywhere, in need of regular reminders of the sources of their convictions. What most sets the Amish apart is their willingness to cultivate those sources in spiritual solidarity with one another.

Nothing about the horror of losing children could, therefore, be reasonably said to be any easier for the Amish than for anyone else. But the path they follow from anger and anguish to forgiveness is somehow more direct than it is for most of us, not easier but simpler. It is well trod and believed to be self-evidently good and right. There is no fundamental need to rethink the issue of whether it is legitimate or justified. Forgiveness is an assumption rather than a distant possibility. The Amish don't forgive in order to lower their heart rates or boost their immune systems. They don't consult Augustine or Aquinas or the other great Christian thinkers. They don't regard it as psychotherapy. It is simple to them because they accept it as the will of God as revealed in the Scriptures, and they rehearse their way into it day after day. That doesn't make it easy.

SEVENTY TIMES SEVEN: A RADICAL, PERSONAL TEACHING

The wellspring of forgiveness for Christians is the person and ministry of Jesus. His example reflects much of what Jews before him believed. He preached a clear message: you have been forgiven by God; therefore, out of gratitude and to complete the circle, forgive others. You are to pass on something much bigger than yourself, which you did not give yourself and whose nature is to move through you to others. Forgiveness is a gift that needs to be given not as a stern rule but as a joyful response. It is a kind of joy that expands precisely where you wouldn't expect it to because you yourself were an unexpected recipient. Forgiveness is about surprise and rebirth. When you say the Lord's Prayer, you ask and promise to "forgive us our trespasses *as we forgive* those who trespass against us." Our reception of forgiveness, then, is a function of our forgiving others. You cannot understand what God's forgiveness of you means without also grasping the power of forgiveness toward others.

Jesus doesn't go around bestowing forgiveness in general, but to particular people. In doing so, he says it is the greatest gift imaginable. His hearers sometimes have other priorities. When the paralytic man is brought to him on a stretcher for healing, Jesus' immediate response is to tell the man his sins are forgiven. The crowd is disappointed. This isn't what they had in mind. They have come to see the man regain his feet. Jesus obliges by restoring the man's ability to walk. Everyone seems satisfied; although most then, as now, probably missed the point. It is worth noting that forgiveness itself didn't bring the man back to full physical health. Perhaps it strengthened his immune system, but to Jesus those effects paled in comparison to the spiritual cleansing he had bestowed. Next to that, any side benefits that might accrue are at best secondary inasmuch as they receive no mention from him.

Over the course of human history, religion has offered perks of its own to coax reluctant forgivers. Penitents might gain nothing less than God's approval and a place in heaven. Whether the would-be forgiver is seeking benefits for selfish reasons or striving selflessly and lovingly to serve the wishes of God is often hard to tell. The secret lies in the unseen designs of the heart. But religious history offers its own enticements, which mirror the goal summed up in the old phrase, "doing well by doing good." It was applied in the past to the rationale of certain robber barons who created gigantic philanthropies that deflected attention from their human abuses and burnished their public reputations.

Although Christian clerics and scholars have added much complexity and fine-tuning to the subject of forgiveness, the core of Jesus' teaching as understood by the Amish remains the model of staggering simplicity and power, the natural confluence between God's forgiveness and ours. There are no limits. Asked how many times we should forgive, Jesus replies, "seventy times seven," which can excite pragmatists eager to fill their merit quotas until it is pointed out that Jesus is using a figure of speech that symbolizes infinity. There is never enough forgiving. On the cross, Jesus takes the lesson one step further by forgiving his executioners and the thief on a nearby cross, a stretching of limits that many have surely found absurd. Forgiveness is always

> "Forgiveness is not an occasional act: it is a permanent attitude."
> —Martin Luther King Jr.

about confounding the conventional wisdom of the world. For Christians, it is available through the most commonplace ritual—baptism— during which the initiate is embraced within the scope of Jesus' death and resurrection.

Religious forgiveness in Christianity and other major world religions begins at the top. It comes, fountain-like, from the deity. Whereas the forgiveness scholars from the human sciences adopt a largely secular outlook, trusting that human beings have the capacity to forgive each other through their own efforts, religious forgiveness flows from a nonhuman source that brings it to life and sustains it. Rather than seeing the distinction as the opposition of science to religion, however, it is perhaps more accurate to see them as complementary. The seekers after scientific results aren't badmouthing the idea of God; they just prefer to keep otherworldly factors out of their thisworldly experiments. The differences in orientation do not preclude similar outcomes.

Without actual belief that God or the gods have made forgiveness available in the first place, the religious appeal falls flat or goes awry. If believers place no actual confidence in that source or in the words they profess, then they are on their own, dependent on their own resources. For many of these forgiveness agnostics, the more secular clinics afford a practical alternative from a humanistic base.

The believers run into potential snags too. Take the prodigal son story, for example, in which the fairness of God's forgiveness is itself troublesome. It is in Luke 15:11-32. The tale is familiar. The father, often seen as a stand-in for God, divides his treasure between his two sons. The older one stays on the ranch and does his duty. Meanwhile, his younger brother takes his share and heads for the city fleshpots, where he overdoes just about everything. It is as if he is on an extended college spring break with nothing more on his mind than satisfying his cravings. "He is into himself," as we would say. But inevitably his luck runs out. He ends up in a pig sty without two coins to his name and, having hit bottom, as it were, decides to hightail it home. Dear old Dad spots him from afar, probably like one of those running-through-the-field commercials, and throws a big bash for him, lavishing pardon and the fatted calf on the delinquent lad. We rejoice. But is all forgiven? There is that older son watching from the wings. He has played it straight and owned up to his responsibility, but his free-love brother gets the royal treatment. Is the older

brother called upon to forgive his younger sibling for skipping town for a round of debauchery? Or should he forgive his father for welcoming his brother too easily? Or both of them, or neither of them? The Gospel story doesn't say. It celebrates the glory of repentance and the freedom it unleashes, but the other half of the story is left for us to ponder. The subtleties and interweaving of who owes what to whom keep the mind astir. In this case, the hearts of the father and the rehabbed prodigal are open, awash in freedom. The older son withholds himself, and most of us sympathize with him, though we also sense that for the sake of himself and his family he needs to escape the dungeon in which resentment has imprisoned him. And whether he can, we intuit, depends on whether he sincerely believes in the reality of God and that that forgiveness is a gift from God. It is a deceptively tall order.

Judaism, Islam, and Hinduism share the view that pardon originates beyond this world. All those traditions necessarily involve questions of personal accountability to the deity and to those who have been wronged. What distinguishes the Christian teaching is how thoroughly personal it becomes through the role of Jesus. While forgiveness in all traditions involves transactions with or on behalf of a supernatural being, Christianity alone claims that God came to earth

Wiesel tries another balance between hatred and anger. He rejects hatred, while reserving a right to be angry. His exposure to the death camps had given him a hatred for the Nazis and alienation from God, he said, but he recently wrote that he'd made peace with the Almighty in a "Letter to God," an op-ed piece in the *New York Times* in celebration of the Jewish New Year. In his background interview for the film, Wiesel testified to that turnabout. "Hate is destructive and therefore I fight hatred," he said, noting that many of those with whom he was liberated came out hating. "So I'm against that," he says. "Anger I'm not [against]. Anger is a good thing."

While Wiesel's insistence that the Holocaust imposes limits on forgiveness is both widely affirmed and debated, there is virtually no disagreement with his view that anger is a natural, necessary prerequisite to any type of healing. To deny the despair and fury over a loved one's violent death at the hands of

---

"Hate is destructive and therefore I fight hatred," he said, noting that many of those with whom he was liberated came out hating. "So I'm against that," he says. "Anger I'm not [against]. Anger is a good thing."

---

another is, in the vast range of forgiveness literature, a crime against one's own nature. The consensus is that anger can help provide the very fuel needed to drive an aggrieved soul beyond hostility to a better place. Even if that comes about, however, the collective wisdom cautions against thinking that anger will vanish. The human psyche has a tendency to recall painful memories and traumatic episodes even after the cause of anger has been forgiven. Though such disruptions may trouble people for the rest of their lives, the emotional reflex is considered both normal and temporary. For the sincere forgiver, the heavier burden of entrenched anger and hatred has been lifted.

In contrast to Catholicism's concept of the Church as the middle agent between God and the penitent, Jews and Protestants think forgiveness involves no intermediaries. Nobody else can process the request or relay the results. It's everyone for himself or herself.

The Jewish manual on the subject might read something like this, with thanks to Rabbi David R. Blumenthal, a professor of Judaic studies at Emory University, whose writings shed bright light on the Jewish approach to forgiveness. From ancient times, when bulls, rams, and other creatures were extinguished in pursuit of God's mercy for the sins of the people, Jewish thinking has evolved and elaborated. The direction of this thought has remained largely the same, however. Among the religious contributions to the topic of forgiveness, Judaism's stands out as the most reasonable and grounded. It mingles the practical with the holy, a forerunner of civil law within the framework of sacred text.

Even a cursory awareness of Judaism since the destruction of the temple in 70 CE makes clear that this is a religious tradition that, since the ancient times of Jewish priests and Temple sacrifices, has removed most institutional layers between believers and God. Today, forgiveness is mainly a matter of direct negotiation without go-betweens. The Jewish manual would contain no mention of confessing to a priest. Neither would it bow to any claim that another human being like a priest could grant forgiveness after confessing. And it would require nothing like a full meeting of hearts and minds between offenders and offended, unless such outcomes were warranted by special circumstances.

Jews provide guidelines to those directly involved in seeking forgiveness as well as those asked to grant it. If repentance is on your mind, you have at your disposal a routine of "return" called *Teshuva*, a series of steps aimed at gaining awareness of personal sins, being sorry for them, sinning no more, paying back the one you've hurt, and confessing to that person.

On the forgiving side, you are reminded that the only one who can start the process is the offender, and only the offended one can let go of the wrong. If the penitent who has stolen your hay wagon asks you for forgiveness three times and you turn a deaf ear, then the sin falls on you. It's an ingenious clause; such limits ideally spur both sides to get on with it. It is intended to cover ordinary person-to-person

---

The ten-day period from the start of Rosh ha-Shana to the end of Yom Kippur is known as *Aseret Y'mai Teshuva*, the Ten Days of Repentance. But the four-step process of repentance applies anytime:

- Step 1—*Regret*: Realize the extent of the damage and feel sincere regret.
- Step 2—*Cessation*: Immediately stop the harmful action.
- Step 3—*Confession*: Articulate the mistake and ask for forgiveness.
- Step 4—*Resolution*: Make a firm commitment not to repeat it in the future.

---

violations like wagon-stealing incidents that, in Jewish thinking, can be settled only by the parties involved in the incident. God cannot forgive the rascal, but the victim can.

Forgiveness is never just forgiveness in religious traditions. Judaism as the parent of the other two great Abrahamic faiths spelled out the basic terms. The first distinction is between the person seeking it and the person granting it.

As noted, the one looking for forgiveness needs to approach the victim hat in hand in Jewish thought. Ask humbly three times; and if there's no response, you've done your duty and the onus is on the victim. The need to tell the victim that you're sorry is pretty much a staple of religious tradition; but Judaism gives it a particularly reasonable definition. With regard to crimes against God, there is no statute of limitations, of course. If you've transgressed the commandment against chasing after false gods (money? prestige?), that blunder will remain a barrier to good relations with God so long as you don't fess up.

From a ground-level perspective, human factors often blunt and overwhelm the higher purposes of religion. Truth may overlap with practicality. While full pardon is held up as the greatest good, Judaism and other faiths recognize a middle ground where a measure of forgiveness can take place in light of extenuating circumstances. The broadest kind of forgiveness in Rabbi Blumenthal's lexicon is to absolve the offender of any debt. If someone has spread malicious gossip about me, I may give up any notion that the perpetrator owes me anything while refusing to erase the bad behavior from my mental record book.

But I may not even want to go that far. As the victim, Jewish thought tells me, I must hold the door open for the offender to make good on the wrong that is done. But if I suspect that the offender is faking sorrow for the offense or hasn't done anything to fix the problem, I can decide to wait until enough rehabilitation has

> From a ground-level perspective, human factors often blunt and overwhelm the higher purposes of religion. Truth may overlap with practicality. While full pardon is held up as the greatest good, Judaism and other faiths recognize a middle ground where a measure of forgiveness can take place in light of extenuating circumstances.

been done before I consider the person forgiven. If the one who has lied about me all over town hasn't shown me evidence that he or she has taken steps to reform sincerely, then I can withhold my gift of forgiveness.

Forgiveness can occur, therefore, without kissing and making up. Even that can happen according to the third variety in Rabbi Blumenthal's typology: unconditional forgiveness—atonement—that comes from God and is impossible on a human level alone. All is forgiven, though the person-to-person resolution of the issues that caused the rupture between or among them must be completed in order for the circle to be complete. The Jewish teaching is especially clear. God cannot erase a transgression done against you by someone else; nor can you cleanse yourself fully of a sin you've committed against someone else without the other's forgiveness.

The gradations of forgiveness permit some good to happen between violator and violated short of the best that could happen. Something becomes better than nothing so long as the something is authentic. The best in religious lore is not possible, however, without the violator pleading for a clean slate or being required to shape up. Religion brilliantly takes into account the hard circumstances, the emotional roadblocks, and the spiritual difficulties that human beings encounter in real life circumstances. The idea that you don't have to proceed immediately to a spiritual zone that is free of anger and resentment can allow victims to take tentative first steps.

The premise is that nobody's perfect except perhaps once in a great while. At the same time, perfection isn't necessary in order to forgive or be forgiven. It is a journey hobbled by vices and foibles. The important thing is that we try. Impaired as we might be, we can either go ahead when we feel ready or fake it until we feel it.

Perfection isn't necessary in order to seek to forgive or be forgiven. It is a journey hobbled by vices and foibles. The important thing is that we try.

Wiggle room is built into these great faiths, at least in their own reckoning of forgiveness as a method of accommodating the needs of conscience. Rabbi Harold Kushner, author of *Why Bad Things Happen to Good People*, offered his own slant on the question of forgiving Nazis. It is a rationale that frees Jews of rage while keeping the Nazi imprisoned in his crime. "What you did was thoroughly despicable and puts you outside the category of decent human beings," Kushner said in *The Sunflower*. "But I refuse to give you the power to define me as a victim. I refuse to let your blind hatred define the shape and context of my Jewishness. 'I don't hate you; I reject you.' And then the Nazi would remain chained to his past and to his conscience, but the Jew would be free."

Attention to one's own personal moral balance sheet is a constant obligation, however. The Jewish prayers recited three times a day, *Amdah*, include this plea: "Forgive us, our father, for we have sinned; pardon us, for we have transgressed." On the highest holy day, the Day of Atonement, the central concept is that God forgives only those who have sought the forgiveness of those they have wronged. Judaism isn't generally comfortable with dispensing forgiveness person-to-person without having done *Teshuva*, the steps undertaken in order to "return" to harmony.

The great Maimonides elaborated on this practice in his "Laws of Forgiveness." They include the following: admission of wrongdoing; confession in public before God and community; open remorse; a public pledge to refrain from such wrong again; restitution to victims and charity to members of the community; up

to three appeals for forgiveness; and shunning those circumstances that gave rise to the wrongdoing.

Whatever their analyses, strategies, and fine-print solutions, the three major branches of Abraham's descendents must wrestle with forgiveness because God, by example, tells them to. Abundant evidence indicates that human followers of these faiths don't much care for this responsibility and will justify their own actions and blame others rather than admit their own perfidy or let someone else "off the hook." No matter how much kicking and screaming, however, the moral imperative of forgiveness remains at the center of Jewish, Christian, and Muslim life. Its claims can be modulated or calibrated to make it more palatable or provisional, but the proverbial 800-pound gorilla stays in the middle of our living room, asking nothing less than what we seem least willing to give, total compliance.

Lest Islam be considered an exception, the precept is ensconced in that tradition as solidly as it is in its sister faiths. One of Allah's 99 names is Al-Ghafoor, the Forgiving One, and the follower of Muhammad is expected to show forgiveness as a sign of fitness for the life beyond. Muhammad displayed it first himself. After his forces gained victory over their foes in Mecca, he treated the rest of its citizens with mercy instead of punishing them. Islam has its own forgiveness calculus, of course. Whereas Jews may stop short of pardoning the Nazis, and Christians of various stripes label certain actions such as the killing of the Amish children "unforgivable," Muslims believe their faith allows them to steer a path between a legitimate degree of retribution and all-out vengeance toward those who have violated them. Their position, couched in terms of justified self-defense and eye-for-an-eye justice, has parallels in Christian just-war theory and Jewish resistance to enemies. All three traditions have an element of a shoot-first-ask-questions-later mentality, which folds clumsily into the forgiveness suitcase. A consistent course would presumably permit the use of force to preserve life and to forgive the aggressor later. Even in such circumstances, however, the pesky call for forgiveness originating with God, Yahweh, or Allah makes its wishes known in absolute terms, however those terms might be fudged. The divine presumption is always for limitless forgiveness; the human condition clamors for exclusions and escape clauses.

Muslims teach that forgiving is essential to reaching a preferred afterlife, as do the other great faiths. No matter how the issue is framed, the road to God is through the exercise of forgiveness. All three traditions say, in their own way, that if you want to be on God's good side you'd best start thinking how. In the Doblmeier film, the Rev. James Forbes, pastor of Riverside Church in New York City, advises his hearers against tackling the tough cases first. "The best way to begin to talk about forgiveness is not to tell folks to forgive their enemies," he counsels. "That is hard as the beginning point. First let them think about how much forgiveness God has had to grant them from their childhood up to their level of maturation. They have had to make withdrawals from the bank of grace many, many times."

Religious literature also cautions against assuming that ethical pratfalls requiring such withdrawals can be avoided simply by obeying a stated set of commandments. Jesus and Rabbi Abraham Joshua Heschel, for example, offer similar versions that illustrate the danger

Muslims teach that forgiving is essential to reaching a preferred afterlife, as do the other great faiths. No matter how the issue is framed, the road to God is through the exercise of forgiveness.

of selective morality and hypocrisy. In Matthew 25, Jesus is depicted as presiding over the final judgment. Those on his right hand have been saved, he says, because "I was hungry and you gave me food, I was thirsty and you gave me drink, I was a stranger and you welcomed me,

---

"I did not bring forgiveness with me, nor forgetfulness. The only ones who can forgive are dead; the living have no right to forget."—Chaim Herzog

---

I was naked and you clothed me, I was sick and you visited me, I was in prison and you came to me." His listeners are startled. They don't remember feeding, welcoming, dressing, or visiting Jesus in jail. His reply for the ages: "Truly, I say to you, as you did it to one of the least of my brethren, you did it to me." Ahhh. He then pronounces damnation on those on his left because they have failed to recognize him in the suffering souls who needed their help. They assure him they would have rushed to assist him—if it had actually been him—but they hoist themselves on their own petard. Celebrity-chasing will get them nowhere so long as those suffering brothers and sisters

Jesus loves and who follow him are ignored. A show of moral earnestness and opportunism has done them in.

Rabbi Heschel's story is among the Simon Wiesenthal collection of Jewish responses to an imaginary Nazi's plea for deathbed forgiveness. Heschel's answer takes the form of a tale about a rabbi of scholarly renown who boards a train in Warsaw for his hometown of Brisk. There he runs into a group of salesmen who don't know him. They try to goad him out of his meditations, irritated by what they regard as his air of superiority. One of them invites the rabbi to play cards and he politely declines. The man grows angrier, then seizes hold of the rabbi and hurls him out of the compartment. They all leave the train at Brisk and as the rabbi arrives his admirers swarm him. The salesman wonders why and is told that the man he assaulted was the famous rabbi of Brisk. He is at once alarmed at having bullied the wrong man. If only he'd known. . . . In an effort to make up for his nasty behavior, he asks the rabbi for forgiveness. The rabbi refuses. Even some members of the synagogue are startled by his refusal. The salesman next recruits the rabbi's son to learn why his father has denied the plea.

"I cannot forgive him," the rabbi replies to his son. "He did not know who I was. He offended a common man. Let the salesman go to [the common man] and ask for forgiveness." The offender would have refrained from insulting a respected rabbi; but now that the rabbi's identity has been revealed, it is too late for the offender to return to the original scene to undo the damage.

Heschel adds: "No one can forgive crimes committed against other people. It is therefore preposterous to assume that anybody alive can extend forgiveness for the suffering of any one of the six million people who perished. According to Jewish tradition, even God Himself can only forgive sins committed against Himself, not against man."

Hindu and Buddhist Insight into *Karma*, Compassion, and Conversion

Buddhists and Hindus espouse the concept of *karma*, which poses a solution to the problem of evil deeds in a vastly different manner. Simply put, the wickedness done by anyone becomes a source of suffering in a next life. The soul continues to carry the debts of previous lives unless and until the soul gains freedom through righteous practice. It is, therefore, an internal settling of accounts that can go on and on until justice comes about. The two great faiths therefore promote the most

eternal variety of self-help, the purification of the soul, contingent upon right practices. Hindus are admonished to forego retaliation and violence lest they bring increased suffering on themselves. For Buddhists, who do fine without a god, the keys to reducing and even ending the soul's misery are forbearance and compassion. Forbearance is the refusal to return violence for violence or hostility for hostility. Compassion means the offended person's ability to feel the suffering of the offender. Both require long and diligent cultivation.

Thich Nhat Hanh, the celebrated Buddhist monk, underscores that lesson in *The Power of Forgiveness*. Compassion and forbearance must be nurtured from the inside rather than imported through willpower. "Forgiveness will not be possible," he said, "until compassion is born in your heart. Even if you want to forgive, you cannot forgive."

The word for it in Western tradition is *conversion*. Without a rebirth in the heart, every effort to be a forgiving person fails by the collective wisdom of the world's religions. Unless the wounded soul is ready to embrace something that otherwise seems so unnatural, nothing seems possible. The intention may help, and openness to a mysterious turnabout can prepare the ground, but the seeding and watering arise from divine sources.

*Thich Nhat Hanh, the celebrated Buddhist monk,
teaches compassion as an antidote to vengeance.*

"I think that forgiveness is not something that you choose to do entirely," Thomas Moore, psychologist and author of *Care of the Soul*, says in the film. "It's not really something that *you* do. I don't think it's an ego activity in that sense. It's not something that you do or I do. It's something that has been evoked. We can't control the dynamic of what forgiveness is. So that means that forgiveness itself by its definition, its essence, is not something that someone does."

He continues in the background interview: "Forgiveness is a condition, or is a state, or it's even a gift. It's a kind of grace, you might say. It's almost a theological thing, a spiritual thing that comes of its own when we have done what is required to allow it to appear. I think we can forgive in a superficial way. We can say, OK, yes, I want to forgive you; you're forgiven. But there's a big difference between that and really feeling the thing. I think the feeling comes first. It's not really an emotion, it's not just an emotion. It's actually a very deep awareness."

The conversion experience is common and ineffable among religious people. Often it is inspired by the examples of spiritual drama and heroism that have flowed in the current of history. Why some testify to it and others don't has invited a host of theories, inquiries, and explanations over the centuries. It seems always to involve seeing behind appearances to fundamental realities that reshape lives, often dramatically. In the religious understanding of forgiveness, all the talk, all the guidebooks, all the pious practices put together count for nothing without this turning of the heart and mind by a process that has no formula.

One thing appears certain: when and if that change in consciousness takes place, anything can happen.

I Am a Witness

Elie Wiesel

Well known throughout the world, Jewish novelist, political activist, Nobel Laureate, and Holocaust survivor Elie Wiesel is the Andrew Mellon Professor of the Humanities at Boston University. He is the author of over 40 books, the best known of which is Night, *a memoir that describes his experiences during the Holocaust and his imprisonment in several concentration camps. What follows are excerpts from Wiesel's address on January 27, 2000, to the German parliament or Bundestag, inaugurating an annual Day of Remembrance for the Victims of the Holocaust.*

I am a witness and I speak to you today with neither bitterness nor hate. All my adult life I have tried to use language to fight hate, to denounce it, to disarm it, not to spread it.

UNDERSTANDING THE UNINTELLIGIBLE

Will my words hurt you? That is not my intention. But please understand, when I entered this Chamber, I did not leave my memories behind. In fact, here, because of you, they are more vivid than ever. All I wish to do in this short time is to evoke in a few words an unprecedented event that will, for generations to come, continue to weigh on the destiny of my people and yours.

And this event, I still don't understand it. I go on trying and trying. Since my liberation, on April 11, 1945, I have read everything I could lay my hands on that deals with its implications. Historical essays, psychological analyses, testimonies and testaments, poems and prayers, assassins' diaries and victims' meditations, even children's letters to God. But though I managed to assimilate the facts, the numbers and the technical aspects of the "*Aktionen*," the implacable significance that transcends them, continues to elude me. The Nuremberg Laws, the anti-Jewish decrees, the *Kristallnacht*, the public humiliation of proud Jewish citizens, including brave World War I veterans, the first concentration camps, the euthanasia of German citizens, the Wannsee conference,

where the highest officials of the land simply met to discuss the validity, the legality and the ways of killing an entire people. And then of course Dachau, Auschwitz, Majdanek, Sobibor—the capitals of this century. Yes, these names . . . flags, black flags, reminding a world that will come, of a world that has been. What made them possible? How is one to comprehend the cult of hatred and death that flourished in this country? How could bright young men, many superbly educated, from fine families, with diplomas from Germany's best universities, which then were the best in the world, how could they allow themselves to be seduced by Evil to the point of devoting their genius, the genius of Evil, to the torture and the killing of Jewish men, women and children whom they had never seen? They didn't do it because these Jews were rich or poor, believers or nonbelievers, political adversaries, patriots or universalists, but simply because they had been born Jewish. Their birth certificate had became a de facto death sentence. But did it really make these killers feel strong and heroic to murder defenseless children? Could they really have been so afraid of old and sick people, of small children as to make them their priority targets? What was it about them that was frightening? Their weakness, their innocence perhaps? Were the killers still human? That is the question that is my obsession. At what point does humanity end? Is there a limit beyond which humanity doesn't deserve its name anymore?

While preparing myself for today's encounter with you—an encounter of course which is symbolic on more than one level, as you put it very well, President of the Bundestag—I reread certain chronicles by survivors and witnesses, both living and dead. And I was struck again by how similar the scenes of cruelty were. It is as though one German, always the same, tortured and killed one Jew, forever the same, six million times. Yet each episode is unique, for every human being, created in God's image, is unique. . . .

Asking for Forgiveness?

I am here, and I remember 55 years ago. I remember, and if I were to tell you what I remember, you would, like me, tremble. So, let us speak rather of what has to be done. I as a Jew, of course, speak of the Jewish victims, my people. Their tragedy was unique, but I do not forget other victims. When, as a Jew, I evoke the Jewish victims, I honor the others as well. As I like to put it: not all victims were Jewish but all Jews were victims.

And it is to remember them, Mr. President, Mr. Chancellor, President of the Bundestag, that this Parliament is marking the 27th of January as a day for commemorating the victims of the Nazi regime or, as I would call it, National Holocaust Remembrance Day. And this decision does you honor. And my presence here is meant, of course, to highlight your willingness to open the gates of memory and to declare together our conviction and resolution that it is high time for Cain to stop murdering his brother Abel.

After the war, some of us expected a defeated and humiliated Germany to deliver a more powerful message of remorse and contrition, one that would be linked to morality; instead, in those years it was related more to politics. But, since Chancellor Konrad Adenauer's time, you have become a democracy, worthy of taking its place in the family of nations. You have consistently supported Israel, and your record of financial reparations to the victims, mainly to the Jewish victims, but also to all slave laborers, as the law you are introducing in Parliament stipulates, is positive. But I believe that perhaps the time has come for you to make a gesture that would have worldwide repercussions.

President Rau, you met a group of Auschwitz survivors few weeks ago. And one of them told me that you expressed something very moving. You asked for forgiveness for what the German people had done to them. Why shouldn't you do it here? In the spirit of this solemn occasion. Why shouldn't the Bundestag simply let this be known to Germany and its allies and its friends, and especially to young people? Have you asked the Jewish people to forgive Germany for what the Third Reich did in Germany's name to so many of us? Do it, and it will have extraordinary repercussions in the world. Do it, and the significance of this they will acquire a higher dimension. Do it, and the world will know that its faith in this Germany is justified. For, beyond national, ethnic or religious considerations, it was mankind itself that was threatened then, in those darkest of days. And in some ways, it still is. Whatever this new century holds in store, and we desperately want to have hope for the new century and its new generation, Auschwitz will continue to force men to explore the deepest recesses of his and her being so as to confront their fragile truth.

I told you before that I prefer stories. I would like to conclude with the story of a little Jewish girl who died with her mother the night they arrived in Birkenau in May 1944. She was eight years old, and believe me, she had done nothing to hurt or harm your people—why did she have to die such an atrocious death? If her brother lives to be as old as the world itself, he will never understand. And so, he will simply quote another great Hasidic Master: Rabbi Moshe Leib of Sassov. He was known for his great compassion and he said: "My friends, do you wish to find the spark? Look for it in the ashes."

Two

Health

Scientific minds have recently joined the pilgrimage to revisit the mysteries of forgiveness. As is their wont, they ask blunt questions about things that can be measured. What happens, if anything, to the physical self as the result of forgiving? How does such an act affect the mind? Evidence so far shows that benefits occur to the forgiver in both areas of personal well-being. Promoting forgiveness for self-gain runs the risk of buttressing an already robust trend toward preoccupation with a variety of new age egotism, however, and thereby neglecting concern for others. But it can also be argued that forgiveness is a welcome outcome, no matter what the motive. Far more dangerous is the man or woman who is mired in death-dealing resentments and rage at wrongs, real or imagined.

Deep in the Watergate morass, Richard Nixon cultivated an "enemies list" comprised of those he thought were out to get him. Whether some or all of the notables in the president's rogues' gallery were actual enemies, Nixon clearly believed he was under attack by an elite corps of politicians, intellectuals, and journalists. He wore his resentments both openly and privately, as the infamous secret tapes reveal. It's possible that in his retirement he had a change of heart and divested himself of these antipathies, but the Nixon the public saw appeared to harbor his real or imagined wrongs until his dying day.

The Forgiveness Science

Research has compiled growing evidence that persons who bottle up their rage and remain unforgiving endanger their health. When Nixon died in 1994, the scientific study of the effects of such behavior was in still in the beginning stages. A decade later, the experiments were spreading rapidly and coming to some impressive findings. Holding on to gripes and accusations can make you sick. Would the remote, unrelenting Nixon have listened to such claims if he had not already made peace with his inner demons? Given what we know about him, the

chances are slim at best, and in that regard he probably resembles a preponderance of human beings. For most of us, changing is nothing less than taking the chisel of good advice to the granite of our character in an effort to reshape basic features. Though it's not popular to say so in polite company, many of us fear that having our anger and "inexcusable" actions chipped away would destroy much of our essential character. Without those familiar, bilious traits, who would we be, and how would we defend ourselves? By this logic, setting aside hatred and condemnation risks weakening the core self. Nixon, the prototype of the bitter man from what we know, apparently thought more or less like that.

An Emerging Field in Social Science

The methods of science are offering different ways of thinking and acting. After some struggle to gain legitimacy and resources under the suspicious gaze of academic research, explorations of how the angry-unforgiving personality (the "Phineas T. Bluster" of "Howdy Doody" fame) may suffer both mental and physical ills are proceeding apace. Dr. Everett L. Worthington, Jr., a psychologist at Virginia Commonwealth

University, notes in *The Power of Forgiveness* that in the seven-year period from 1998, when the field was at the take-off point, until 2005, the number of forgiveness studies jumped from 58 to 950, more than a sixteen-fold increase. It was gaining respect from the skeptical scientific club, though some of the leaders of the new study, such as Worthington, were unprepared to claim their findings as scientific fact.

The acknowledged pioneer of this emerging discipline is Dr. Robert D. Enright, a developmental psychologist at the University of Wisconsin at Madison, who is featured in the film as the teacher of reconciliation in Northern Ireland. Enright began looking into the subject in the mid-1980s in the face of opposition from

both religion and academia. He persisted, and over time, and with assistance from the Templeton Foundation, which has funded many of the projects, serious scholars from such respected universities as Virginia Commonwealth, Stanford, Wisconsin, Michigan, Harvard, Case Western, George Mason, and Tennessee have joined the cause. Most participants regard a major research conference in Atlanta in October 2003, sponsored by Templeton and Fetzer, as the time when the various individual efforts melded into something like a discipline with its own identity and momentum.

Participants in the conference reflected the diversity of the budding field. Some presenters had taken a scientific route, attaching electrodes

Dr. Robert D. Enright, a developmental psychologist, has been the prime mover in placing forgiveness studies on the nation's academic agenda.

Asians across the narrow Bering Strait to North America. The continent has been the destination for people who saw it as a starting place rather than a resting place. Self-reliance and striving for personal potential form the national creed, so it is little wonder that whatever promotes those ends, from motivational speeches to herbal remedies to non-verbal prayer, has a ready audience. It fuels fantastic achievements in a host of endeavors. Built into this faith is a drive to conquer whatever impediments get in the way of personal fulfillment, and nothing poses more of an obstacle than ill health. The pursuit of health is perfectly natural on its own, apart from any desire for self-improvement; but in our society it has an especially intimate connection with worldly success as well. We are a famously practical people, and that characteristic has won us deserved fame for problem-solving and fabulous inventions. Not surprisingly, this image of ourselves becomes utilitarian. We view ourselves as functioning units of production who require resources to stay in good running condition for the sake of, yes, self-improvement. This is where

> "To forgive is to set a prisoner free and discover that the prisoner was you."
> —Lewis Smedes

resources such as prayer and the practice of forgiveness can be seen as valuable adjuncts to low-fat diets and daily exercise, the means of fixing the machine for better performance. Bad habits surely account for much of the problem, but not all. Another huge factor is ill effects caused by the fiercely competitive, stressful work climate itself. For many, self-help therapies, rather than taking aim at the destructive effects of the bigger systems themselves, become the response to the crisis. What we often choose to do is to fix broken people in order to send them back into the fray. We patch them up in psychological and spiritual emergency rooms and send them back out. The therapies may provide valuable relief, but the source of the trouble remains so central to our way of life that we dare not name it, let alone touch it.

It also makes sense that emphasis on personal well-being would escalate during a time when so many feel powerless. Polls, surveys, and common sense observation make clear that a growing number of Americans believe they have little or no control over the mega-forces that shape their lives. The relatively low turnout of voters in elections is a major indicator of that mood of futility. The blur of major events in merciless procession on cable television overwhelms and dismays viewers across the nation. That flood of disasters, scandals, wars, and threats is both a proper exercise of news reporting and a monster that drives many people into the only sanctuary they know: themselves. Within the boundaries of their own existence, they have some authority to decide how they attempt to treat their sufferings and enhance their joys. No wonder, then, that the services of self-help become even more sought at a time when the self feels less confident that help will come from anywhere else. At the same time, a spike in interest in something often indicates the absence of that very thing. A focus on death, for example, may indicate less acceptance of it. The heightened interest in religion as a powerful American influence, and how it allegedly shapes politics, is likely a sign of the opposite state—whereby religion has in fact ebbed as a commitment that challenges all areas of life from money to motherhood.

Within that overall cult of the self, the blessing and bane of our national life, the social scientists studying forgiveness are rendering a great service. As the religious appeal for forgiveness has appeared to lose punch and credibility on strictly spiritual terms, and as the coarseness of a society marked by racial divides, gender-role conflict, and political polarization becomes more destructive, the new scholars of forgiveness have taken initiatives to build a scientific rationale for the practice. In most cases, they are therapists as well as scholars who were led to this research as a means of easing emotional pain and suffering. For the most part, they don't reject religious belief or seek to replace it; they rather take a scientific, largely secular tack in searching for methods of healing. On the empirical scale, of course, a large part of that search entails looking for the physical markers that show progress or the lack of it.

In the end, the forgiveness scholars are much more intently concerned with ends rather than means. They generally welcome any religious means toward a valid scientific outcome, which remains the benchmark of credibility. Some have developed strategies of their own for helping clients toward forgiveness, but those methods don't ordinarily deny the value of spiritual traditions, For the most part, the social scientists want to know how people actually do forgive and the effect it has on them.

Looming over this whole upsurge of interest in promoting forgiveness is an increase in what might be called a get-even mentality. To refer to an earlier point, a sudden flurry of concern about some aspect of daily existence can be a sure sign that the thing itself is mostly gone. The recent cry for building "community," for example, signaled the demise of small-town and city-neighborhood connectedness. The myriad programs designed to instill intimacy between lovers was a leading indication of what had largely disappeared. Likewise, an obsession with "security" and safety mirrors not only fear of real dangers but also a loss of the traditional understanding that security is finally unobtainable in the face of death. So it seems with the attractiveness of forgiveness. Fascination with it and study of it shot up as its appeal as a real-life option for overcoming hatred and grievances waned. No matter what the health benefits, a public bent on exacting retaliation on battlefields, courtrooms, highways, and athletic fields, galvanized by big-screen avengers, rough-house cops, and "total" combat in the ring, will be unlikely to welcome an invitation to forgiveness. The advantages of letting go to help the self hit a wall at death row, where powerful instincts of self-protection and societal protection kick in. As the forgiveness scholars themselves note, forgiveness is widely perceived as the response of the wimp, the weak, and the scared. By contrast, the polls register huge majorities in favor of capital punishment and tough sentencing of offenders. Odds are that forgiveness has always been counter-cultural to a degree; to choose that

direction these days is also, broadly speaking, also counter-intuitive.

MEMORY AND MYSTERY

Most of us draw a line somewhere in the sand for certain crimes we won't forgive. No people have been challenged more in this regard than the Jews. As we have seen, many believe that forgiving the Nazis for the horrors of the Holocaust is impossible because, among other reasons, it would detract from the reality of six million murdered Jews. The monstrous nature of that slaughter removes it from such consideration. In its aftermath, some have even refused to pardon for atrocities under God's watch. Responding to a hypothetical question of whether a Jewish slave labor prisoner should forgive an S.S. officer who pleaded for pardon for murdering a man, the noted Jewish writer Cynthia Ozick replied, "Forgiveness is pitiless. It forgets the victim. It drowns out the past. The face of forgiveness is mild, but how stony to the slaughtered. . . ." (quote from *Time* magazine, March 22, 1999, cover story). In the Doblmeier film, Elie Wiesel echoes that limit on forgiveness of Holocaust commanders. In a speech to the Bundestag, he relays an invitation to the German people to ask the Jews for forgiveness for crimes done by the Nazis during the Holocaust. The Bundes president responded to Wiesel's suggestion by doing exactly that in an appearance before the Israeli Knesset. While the issue awaits further resolution, the religiously-laden symbolism of each leader seeking to heal the hideous wounds by visiting a hallowed home of the other itself sent a powerful message.

The forgiveness scholars beg to make a point right here. Please, they insist, separate forgiving someone who has wronged you with your legal right to expect that person to be held accountable by the law. Forgiving is not to be confused with excusing or forgetting or exonerating, they insist. The process of cleansing oneself from vengeance and fury against someone who has caused you harm may take a long time and happen in fits and starts, they say, but it isn't intended to wipe away the offenses or take the violator off the legal hook. It is a more mysterious pathway that can leave both parties less burdened by inner and outer pain. Many intertwine forgiveness with doing justice.

Alexandra Asseily, a Lebanese psychotherapist, has tried to strike such a balance in the wake of her country's gruesome civil war (1975–90), fueled largely by hatred between Christians and Muslims. She appears in the Doblmeier film as a principal backer of a Garden of Forgiveness in Beirut whose purpose would be to help bring healing. Asseily has come through the bloodshed with tough-minded realism about forgiveness and forgetting.

Alexandra Asseily has applied her faith and her insights as a psychotherapist to promote a forgiveness garden to bring together Lebanon's Christians and Muslims.

"On the one hand," she said, "we all talk about peace and we'll have campaigns for peace ta-da, ta-da, but I think most of us don't realize how difficult it is to get peace if we don't pass through that tiny gate which has got lots of barbed wire around it and is extremely difficult to go through—forgiveness."

She continued, "Forgiveness allows us to actually let go of the pain in the memory. And if we let go of the pain in the memory *we can have the memory but it doesn't control us* [emphasis added]. I think it's the fact that when memory controls us we are then the puppets of the past. . . . I believe in remaining connected to our memories, but that they don't drive us with their pain."

EARLY EVIDENCE SUGGESTS BENEFITS TO MIND AND BODY

So what have the lab coats found so far?

The most solid result is that forgiving yourself and others can be a bonanza for your heart and your blood vessels. Blood pressure goes down, therefore easing the workload on the cardio-pumper. Researchers have conducted scores of tests to measure the change in pressure when subjects are asked to remember a person or incident that has caused the person anger and distress. Compared to an unforgiving person, the forgiving subject may also show a rise in pressure, but it generally peaks at a lower level and falls more rapidly. This effect is as sure

as any conclusion in the field. Blood pressure drops as forgiveness increases. As in all science, this conclusion is held open to possible revision in light of new discoveries, but it has held up well and offers hope to those with life-threatening hypertension. The message: you hold on to your gripes at peril of a heart attack or a stroke. The effect of forgiveness on a growing number of other maladies is also being tested. In addition to abused women and drug addicts, subjects have been victims of spinal injuries, lower back pain, HIV/AIDS, and divorce. Predictably, perhaps, forgiveness has also become a staple of many marriage therapists.

Closely related to this physical boon is evidence that forgiveness can reduce or prevent emotional disorders such as anxiety, neuroses, and depression. Dr. John Maltby, a psychologist at the University of Leicester in England, has been a leading investigator in this area. Forgiving oneself can contribute to mental health as much as or more than forgiving others, Maltby says. His conclusions have been reinforced by many other studies. If you can do your heart a favor by forgiving, the efforts by Maltby and his colleagues indicate that your psyche may get a boost at the same time.

Forgiving the self has been receiving lots of attention both as a method of untangling emotional knots that can be crippling and as a process of liberating oneself from the slave of vengeance. While scholars and therapists believe it can be an enormously helpful process, however, they caution that it is often hard to achieve and that the process itself can mask ego inflation.

A leading researcher in this area has described how "easy" forgivers can subvert more benign intentions. Dr. Jane Tangney of George Mason University thinks she has discovered that among those most ready to give themselves a break exists a category of egomaniacs. She makes this stunning assessment in the abstract of her research paper on the topic, asserting that "people who easily forgive themselves appear to be rather self-centered, insensitive, narcissistic individuals who come up short in the moral emotional domain, showing lower levels of shame, guilt, and empathetic responsiveness."

Her abstract continues, "Relatively 'shameless,' they feel little remorse for their transgressions, little empathy for their victims, and little concern about what others think of them. Although quick to forgive themselves, they're harsh in response to others' transgressions.

"These characteristics of self-forgiving individuals may cause distress to those around them. But self-forgivers are themselves unfazed.

The propensity to forgive the self was positively correlated with self-reports of psychological well-being, and negatively correlated with internal psychological distress. Only clinical problems associated with a lack of self-control (e.g., drugs and alcohol abuse) were positively correlated with self-forgiveness. In short, self-forgivers may act 'bad' but they don't feel bad."

Tangney's conclusions offer a startling illustration of how complex the forgiveness field can be. Her observations add a different dimension to the discussion without negating or debunking the chorus of therapist-researchers who sing the praises of self-forgiving. But her work is a reminder the illusive, tricky nature of diagnosing inner states of mind. Thus, a display of self-forgiving may contribute to a sounder mind and sounder body, or do either, or neither. Further, the quality of sincerity may be difficult to measure even with the devices available to pick up metabolic changes. As Tangney notes, the narcissists among her subjects were likely to show no signs of physical or emotional distress.

> "I never had more to forgive as when I began my studies of forgiveness."
> —Robert D. Enright

attain a considerable level of peace with the ones who have betrayed them. In a background interview for the film, Lawler-Row said her curiosity about forgiveness was piqued in 1998 while she was probing the psychological factors that cause heart disease and cancer, especially anger and hostility. After a talk to a group of insurance executives, a man asked her what he was supposed to do with his cooped up anger, because he didn't feel he could either let it out or keep it in. "And I didn't really have a good answer for him," she said. She looked for one, examining the factors affecting scores of students and adults, using the medical testing devices needed to display fluctuations in their metabolism. Like some other researchers, she blends these physical indices with the results of questionnaires completed by the subjects themselves.

Eight years later, she said the "most overarching finding is that every time we measure forgiveness it is associated with positive health.

The more forgiving people have lower blood pressure. They are less aroused during stress. They recover from thinking about this [betrayal] experience more quickly. When we look at survey samples and a variety of measures of health and fatigue, sleep, physical symptoms, number of medications, in every case the more forgiving the person the better their health."

Just how someone becomes a forgiving person remains largely unknown. Those like Lawler-Row who bring people from resistance to acceptance of forgiveness say a lot depends on their ability to put themselves in the shoes of the alleged offenders; but not everybody has the aptitude, disposition, willingness or skill to do that. Enright, like many of his colleagues, thinks willpower alone fails to soften the heart. Once asked if he thought the forgiveness trait might be rooted in biology, perhaps in a "forgiveness gene," he said wasn't qualified to answer but noted that people around the world have a com-

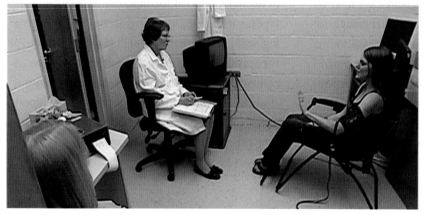

Dr. Lawler-Row, shown with a test subject, has conducted breakthrough experiments in the field.

mon understanding of what forgiveness means, as if to say that it appears somehow inbred.

Lawler-Row and Warren Jones of the University of Tennessee prudently sidestepped the causes and went straight to results. Together they developed survey tools to identify the "forgiving personality," which is generally inclined to let go of anger and accusation, and "acts of forgiveness"

Women were found to score higher as general forgivers, but men more often put it into practice in real cases.

---

which occur in people less forgiving overall but who act that way in particular cases. Subjects were asked to recall painful experiences inflicted by others and were monitored by the standard blood pressure cuffs and, in some studies, devices to track muscle tension and electronic skin conduction. They also responded to a 36-question survey to assess their view of themselves.

Their results, as might be expected, bolster the live-and-let-live cause. Forgiving personalities register lower blood pressure, smoke less, drive better, and generally take better care of their health than their dyspeptic neighbors.

Women were found to score higher as general forgivers, but men more often put it into practice in real cases. Another discovery: the tendency to forgive increases with each succeeding decade of life, challenging the image of the aging, crotchety, "set-in-their-ways" Phineas T. Blusters. All of these categories place subjects on a spectrum, of course, rather than seeing anyone as purely one or the other.

Being a forgiving type on the Lawler-Row and Jones scale doesn't necessarily mean living in an anger-free zone. The researchers emphasize that all-around forgivers are just as prone to be offended as anyone else, but less apt to blow their proverbial stacks, finding less damaging ways to release anger. It's just that they set it aside and channel it in different directions. They describe that alternative road as involving both ridding themselves of the bitterness and developing a degree of good will toward those who have hurt them. Those are two very big corners to turn, but Lawler-Row and Jones say they have seen it happen. And what has been the cause of most of the harm incurred by the students they have studied? It's essentially the stuff of television soaps: love triangles, the double dealing of friends, and the lingering effects of divorce. The cruelest blows are acts of betrayal by those we love and trust the most. They are therefore the hardest to treat.

But Lawler-Row, who advocates the movement of "positive psychology," has become convinced that "if you're a forgiving person and we take into account your healthy behavior and social support that forgiveness gives you, you seem to be associated with a greater sense of purpose in life."

Enthusiastic Proponents Remain Cautious Scientists

To some in the physical sciences, this portrayal of a cause-and-effect relationship may appeal as a mingling of philosophy, theology, and psychology but fall far short of employing either the methods or the verification of strict empiricism. While the intuition and elements of reason resonate with the theory and even the provisional findings, the mind of science remains understandably ambivalent, especially regarding the nonmaterial, value-laden assumptions built into much of the field. The responses among scientists predictably range from dismissal of the whole field as hokum to curiosity and tentative support.

It all depends, too, on who feels it necessary to prove what to whom. Many of the leading forgiveness scholars like Enright say they are satisfied that the blending of physical and psychical elements has produced a solid body of credible findings that has an authority of its own without having to meet the standards of hard science. They say they're prepared for the long haul.

None appears better prepared for pressing ahead than Worthington. As a professor, he apprises his students at Virginia Commonwealth of the latest thinking in the research studies. As a clinician, he employs an "empty chair" method to help those who come to him, including students, to cross from anger to forgiveness. But, remarkably, he serves those two functions as a scholar and therapist whose shared theories about the subject were tested most severely by the horrors of his personal life. His aging mother was brutally murdered by an intruder, and partly as a result of that tragedy, his brother committed suicide. His struggle parallels that of many people he sees with similar troubles. As he explains in the film, the first report of the murder said the assailant had beat his mother again and again until she died. He later learned that she had remained alive for a long time. The murder plunged him into fits of anger. It also sent him down a new road, turning from marriage counseling to exploring forgiveness and justice.

After the brutal death of his mother, he told Doblmeier, "I realized that I think God put me on earth to study forgiveness, to talk with people about it and to do so within the context of justice. That it's not just about forgiveness but about the way forgiveness and justice blend together. That's my mission in life—to bring forgiveness into every willing heart, home, and homeland. But it's forgiveness within the context of doing social justice. Of affirming criminal and civil justice and doing right and using all the procedures. And [seeking] personal justice between people. Forgiving is not opposed to justice. Forgiveness works hand in hand with justice, and I think if understood correctly each spurs the other on."

Years after the murder, Worthington said he has forgiven the man thought responsible, though he has never been brought to trial because of flaws in the legal process. More difficult has been to forgive himself, he said, for his feeling of letting down his brother, who was traumatized at finding their mother dead.

In the laboratory, Worthington is a stickler for scientific techniques used by others in the field to monitor such things as vital signs, skin moisture, and the stress hormone cortisone in the saliva, as well as the personal inventories to detect self-reported moods and traits. His empty chair routine involves creating conversation between the resentful person and alleged offender, who is imagined sitting in that chair, then reversing the process. Worthington is serious about his role as a scientist and, in that capacity, goes to great lengths to verify results. He calls it "triangulation," which consists of comparing what a subject says or does on surveys or in the therapeutic setting with the results displayed by the medical devices. A subject who claims to be at peace yet shows an elevated heart rate, for example, would likely attract Worthington's attention for further examination. It can work both ways, he added.

The murder of his mother led Dr. Everett Worthington (seated second from left among his students) to shift to forgiveness studies.

Sometimes the biological signs indicate low levels of unforgiveness while the person reports being at peace. But more often it's the opposite; someone reports a mood of serenity but shows considerable agitation on the biological charts.

His deep regard for the scientific side of his work leads him to apply tough standards to the findings in the wider field of forgiveness studies. "I always tell my students, never trust a study," he said. "We never trust a study in science. What we trust is the body of studies. If researchers from all over the place with different assumptions and different agendas come at this in different directions and come up with the same findings, we can take that to the bank. I think that's where we've gotten in the field of forgiveness."

At the same time, he said, "I don't think we've established that forgiveness actually helps people be healthier in a way that science would be willing to say this is absolutely established fact. What we've established is that many studies point in that direction, but scientists need to get the white coats on, go in there with the microscope, figure out what happens, how does it happen, what happens in the brain."

The probes into such questions continue apace, as does the broadening of the scope of the field. If doing high-risk research is a sign of the movement's growing confidence, forgiveness science is showing vitality. One recent study, for instance, stretched the dimensions of this research by testing the hypothesis that mentally ill criminals could grow to have empathy for their victims. The subjects, confined in Mendota Mental Health Center in Madison, Wisconsin, volunteered for a one-year forgiveness program that focused, first, on their willingness and ability to forgive someone who had abused them. That recollection of being a victim allowed some to understand the experience of their victims. Mara Alper, a filmmaker who witnessed the program, told the *Christian Science Monitor* that inmates rid themselves of anger by forgiving those who had harmed them. "They felt much calmer, much slower to anger, and able to deal better day to day with their emotions. They are still, though, finding it hard to forgive themselves."

GLIMPSES OF OUR OWN NATURE, ONE CASE AT A TIME

Something about the possibility of forgiving something or someone summons a basic human curiosity. Perhaps it is because we either conjure up a worst-case scenario that seems to us beyond redemption or because we become awestruck when it is reported, wishing we had whatever it might take to achieve that in our own lives.

For most of us, it comes down to cases. We hear the testimony of someone who claims to have forgiven another, usually someone whose story we are drawn to even as we deny the ability to do it ourselves, and we react by being transfixed by it. There is something about forgiveness that compels attention whether we think it miraculous or foolhardy. The most prominent messengers of these alluring stories of personal and national efforts to forgive are the band of social-science troubadours whose foundations are largely secular—self-help and human potential—rather than religious.

A recent "Voices in the Family" program on National Public Radio illustrates the fascination with forgiveness and the sources of its magnetism. The program was on forgiveness; and its host, Dr. Dan Gottlieb, a psychotherapist, explored the topic with Enright, who said the process required both the humility to realize the depth of the hurt and the decision to seek forgiveness. Gottlieb also spoke with a man named Jim LaRue, whose 25-year-old daughter had been raped and murdered on a hiking trip. The man convicted of the crime received the death penalty but was granted a re-sentencing hearing on grounds that proper procedure hadn't been followed. LaRue said that for years he and his wife had been torn by their emotions over their loss. They'd looked toward forgiving the murderer because they opposed the death penalty, but they had been unable to go the whole way. The deciding factor, he said, was coming to accept the belief that every human being has value. A call-in listener said he had been on the roadway in training for a bicycle race when a car traveling at 70-miles-per-hour smashed into him, leaving his bones in pieces and his life one of constant pain since. He had forgiven the driver, he said.

Equally gripping was what happened to Gottlieb himself, who had an epiphany while hosting the program. He suddenly felt a need to rid himself of anger against a man who, he told his radio listeners, had been his best friend long ago. They had lost contact 27 years before, after Gottlieb suffered a terrible accident that cost him permanent use of his legs. The man had never again spoke to Gottlieb, with whom he had shared the adventures of family life and recreation on the golf course and racquetball court. Word came back to Gottlieb that the friend had been too frightened to handle the trauma and chose to avoid facing the consequences. Gottlieb said he had harbored righteous anger and indignation against the man for many years but wrote to him a few years ago with an "at arm's length" attitude. Then, in the midst of the broadcast, the urgency of this unfinished business hit him.

"I wasn't aware of it," he said, "until right now."

Forgiveness as a Field of Inquiry

An Interview with
Robert D. Enright

Robert D. Enright is a Professor of Educational Psychology at the University of Wisconsin-Madison and co-founder of the International Forgiveness Institute, a nonprofit organization dedicated to the dissemination of knowledge about forgiveness and community renewal through forgiveness. He is a licensed psychologist and author of several books, including Forgiveness Is a Choice: A Step-by-Step Process for Resolving Anger and Restoring Hope *(2001).*

AN EVOLVING DISCIPLINE

I was hired at the University of Wisconsin at Madison in 1978 to study moral development in children, or how they change in coming to be fair, decent citizens. By 1985 I had grown weary of the concept of moral development as it was being discussed at that point. The focus was on justice, and I didn't see it as having a major impact on people's lives. So I started looking for something that was unique, potentially helpful to people and something that really could be a line of work for years to come. So I centered on forgiveness. I then looked around at all the psychology journals that I could find at the time, and there were no scientific studies on the topic of forgiveness at all.

I thought maybe this might be a career. So I formed a group of well-meaning, intelligent graduate students from all over the world. We met for Friday morning seminars, starting in the spring of 1985, and that seminar ran for seventeen years. And in that time we asked such questions as, "What is forgiveness? How do you go about forgiving? And what happens scientifically, measurably when people forgive?" And that has been the essence of my career since then.

The interest level within universities in 1985 was such that they thought I had lost my mind. Academics were highly critical of this work thinking that something that is so often mushy and ridiculous as forgiveness had no place at a hard-headed academy, especially a major research university. So I was held up to indifference and scorn and misunderstanding. Quite frankly, I never had more to forgive as when I began my studies of forgiveness.

Now forgiveness is well established as a scientific, foundational area of moral development. Most people who at least take a peak under the tent of forgiveness will realize that the scientific studies show meaningful results with emotionally healthy people, once they forgive. Many people, I would say thousands across the world, are now scientifically studying forgiveness. Yes, there still are skeptics. There always will be, thinking that forgiveness has no place in the hallowed halls of academia. I strongly disagree with that. I have laid my career on the line for the topic, and it's wonderful to see so many people now scientifically studying this topic.

Forgiveness in Scientific Perspective

An Interview with
Kathleen Lawler-Row

Kathleen A. Lawler-Row is Professor of Psychology and Chair of the Department of Psychology, East Carolina University, Greenville, North Carolina. Author of many studies of forgiveness and health, and a Fellow of the American Psychological Society, Dr. Lawler-Row received the 2003 University Studies award for outstanding contributions to interdisciplinary scholarship.

The Studies

In my own research I've been interested in psychological factors and how they predict health and illness. In the past ten years people have shifted to this whole field of positive psychology, trying to understand what kind of factors lead someone to be healthy and to have a high quality of life. Forgiveness has been a part of that discussion.

Initially I wanted to see was there any relationship between forgiveness and physiological response during stress and to health in general. And so I started with college-age population.

We looked at maybe 110 students. And I did a study very much like the first one with middle-aged adults, and there were eighty of those. Then we looked at a group of much older people between fifty and ninety-two. I think there were almost four hundred people in that study. And every one of those showed a connection between forgiveness and health measured in a variety of different ways. So then I moved to try to understand what are the pathways. What is forgiveness doing to someone or for someone that would have an impact on health? That second round of studies has probably been another two or three hundred people.

THE FINDINGS

The most overarching finding is that every time we measure forgiveness, it is associated with positive health. Looking in the laboratory we find that the more forgiving people have lower blood pressures. They are less aroused during stress. They recover off thinking about this experience more quickly. When we look at surveys samples and a variety of measures of health, fatigue, sleep, physical symptoms, number of medications, in every case the more forgiving the person, the better their health.

There are really two parts to forgiveness. There is the letting go of the negative aspect as you think about the other person and how you feel. But there is also positive wishing the other person well. That's probably the other part of forgiveness, having some compassion for the offender or trying to see them in a little more complex light. They are not just the bad thing they did to you; there's also a good piece to them.

In terms itself separate from health, it's been interesting to see that people seem to get a little more forgiving with about every decade in life. With college students, starting at eighteen, there's certainly a wide range of forgiveness. But with each decade the average level of forgiveness goes up. People get a little bit more and a little bit more forgiving, regardless of personality. They just seem to be a little more ready to forgive the other person with age.

Three

Impossible

Whatever physical and spiritual benefits forgiveness may promise, it isn't terribly popular. Thoughts of forgiveness may stir around in our heads, and we may even keep a list of candidates for forgiveness, but one thing or another holds us back. The purpose of this chapter isn't to nag about those unfulfilled intentions but to allow for cases where the refusal to forgive might be understandable or even morally respectable.

This book and *The Power of Forgiveness* film obviously tilt in favor of forgivers. Forgiveness is pitched as a good idea for untangling your innards and patching things up with God— the highly recommended elixir. In daily life, however, forgiveness is the exception rather than the rule. More often we waffle and excuse ourselves from going in that direction because it doesn't feel exactly right. Something similar happens after being instructed to get more exercise. It isn't a simple good-bad thing, as if those who do forgive are right and those who don't are wrong. Determining what's good for you involves all sorts of variables, such as time and even the will of God.

THE LIMITS OF MERCY, HUMAN AND DIVINE

Even Jesus didn't simply forgive all comers. "I say to you," he tells his followers, "all sins and all blasphemies that people utter will be forgiven them. But whoever blasphemes against the Holy Spirit will never have forgiveness, but is guilty of an everlasting sin." (Mark 3:28-29) On other occasions, he condemns those who harm the innocent and vulnerable. With reference to those who threaten the faith of children, for example, he awesomely declares that

"Whosoever causes one of these little ones who believe in me to sin, it would be better for him to have a great millstone hung around his neck and to be drowned in the depths of the sea."

Strong stuff. Forgiveness isn't unconditional in the Gospels. Jesus proclaims judgment even though he may have paid a price for doing so. In his example, it clearly isn't stubbornness or mindless anger that causes him to limit the scope of forgiveness. We might indulge in gratuitous resentment, but we can scarcely image that he did. Exceptions, then, can be honorable.

That leads to hell. The idea that a grim eternity awaits the damned is, of course, a very old idea that hasn't been lost despite the earnest efforts of the Anglican Bishop J. A. T. Robinson to dismiss it as a vestige of a prescientific three-tiered universe. Hell has been understood as the destination of those who fail God's test. As my son reminds me, if everyone were forgiven and waved on into heaven, there would be no hell. In this schema, however, God doesn't award free E-Z passes. Some presumably don't qualify because they simply haven't asked for forgiveness or have done things for which they are not forgiven. They may be caught in an endless cycle of agony by having to live with their sins, even as the

Greek mythological figure Tantalus cannot successfully reach the grapes above him because the water rises to drown him every time he tries. If, as my son says, we are called upon to imitate God in loving, forgiving ways, aren't we also required on occasion to imitate God's refusal to forgive? Hell only makes sense as a pit where God tosses the unforgiven.

Even if you don't believe in a literal hell, you probably feel some need to account for the principle of godly justice. The biblical prophets stomped around denouncing corruption and the treatment of the poor and oppressed in the name of God. From that and a raft of commandments we deduce a system of right and wrong. By those standards, some behavior is so grotesque and so abominable that we'd expect from the divine justice concept that those who act that way would be held accountable to the point of losing any ability to gain forgiveness. In Matthew 25, as we saw, Jesus depicts the separation of sheep from goats. It is not good to be a goat, because that means having violated the law of love for which there will be some form of eternal punishment, whether it be hell or something else. Striving to live justly wouldn't mean much if it didn't matter in the end what you did. If God fires up Jeremiah and Isaiah and Amos and the others to warn the people about their injustices, it seems likely that God rates at least some of that vile behavior as unforgivable. If Stalin, Chairman Mao, Saddam Hussein, Adolf Hitler, or Idi Amin were to get off scot-free, even if they confessed

---

> If we are called upon to imitate God in loving, forgiving ways, aren't we also required on occasion to imitate God's refusal to forgive?

---

to every single hideous crime, that outcome wouldn't comport with the God most of us have come to know. There would appear to be something profoundly wrong with divine fairness and reasoning, however mysteriously we may conceive God.

Without always saying so explicitly, therefore, Western tradition has made room for those who refuse to forgive for various reasons—the unforgivers.

MAKING ROOM FOR PRINCIPLED UNFORGIVERS

Sometimes the monstrous nature of a crime itself becomes an insurmountable obstacle. Genocide and mass killing in Armenia, that they owed me an apology. But that's the way I took it and still do.

In 2004, the cycle ended. The New Yorkers lost to my team (which by then was nearly as rich and powerful itself) in the run-up to the World Series. That turnabout might have calmed the waters. Maybe it was time to bury the madness, forgive them for things they weren't aware they'd done to me, and walk away with a lighter soul. But I haven't budged and don't intend to. It gives me vitality (psychotherapists note: underlying drives are being purposely ignored here). It does my metabolism no good but helps me remember who I am and where I came from. In addition, it's allowed me to belong to a people, a tribe of New Englanders with a common memory. We feed off of it even as we remember its sources in the monumental defeats of the late 1940s. I once almost fell for the line a few years ago that they had become a bunch of nice guys that I couldn't really hate any more. Fortunately, my bile remembers even when I'm tempted to relent. It is among my unapologetic hatreds.

That experience naturally blurs some definitions. It is trifling at the same time that it seems typical. Surrogate hatreds conducted by proxies and distant, perceived offenses, as exist in this case, cannot compare to the aftermath of crimes committed against loved ones and betrayals that humiliate us. There is a common thread between the minor and major forms, however. It is instinctive to store grievances and to protect them against pressures to give them up too cheaply. Resentments and hatreds crop up from a variety of offenses against us (both real and imagined), but once they register we must do something about them. Usually that means keeping them or letting them go. The direction we take depends on many factors, not the least of which, as mentioned earlier, is if the offender has asked us for forgiveness. We may find a way to let go because we expect to gain emotional and spiritual stability. Though achieving that end may prove difficult, a larger motive moves us toward that end. There are also situations, too, where we either cannot or won't surrender to that purpose. These are the "never" cases we may choose to take to the grave.

Jeffrie Murphy runs counter to most forgiveness scholars by arguing that holding on to feelings of anger and revenge can be good medicine. Murphy, a professor of philosophy and law at the University of Arizona, makes his unorthodox, scholarly position in two recent books, *Getting Even: Forgiveness and Its Limits* and *Before Forgiving: Cautionary Views of Forgiveness in Psychotherapy* (with Sharon Lamb). He isn't against forgiveness, but believes it should be exercised cautiously and sparingly. His main contention is that reactive, vengeful emotions often help victims to defend and respect themselves. In academic circles, Murphy runs against the grain by asserting that bitter feelings have a more constructive role than has been acknowledged in most of the current forgiveness trends, but his conclusions, I'm guessing, are close to those of the general public.

If our conscience is our guide, then every candidate for unforgiveness deserves special attention, except when the circumstances shatter all normal categories. Among the examples of overwhelming evil was the Nazi Holocaust, which, as we've discussed, resulted in a reflexive denial of forgiveness by so many Jews, such as Elie Wiesel in the Doblmeier film. This wholesale murder required Judaism to go beyond its long forgiveness tradition. Holding back (though not necessarily "hating") preserves a strain of Jewish dignity. Lest forgiving be confused with condoning or excusing, better not to forgive. Not forgiving helps one retain moral strength in the face of annihilation; it proclaims that the Jewish

people have survived. Some Jews remain angry at God or at the God in whom they were taught to believe for failing to save those consigned to the death camps.

Similar resistance to a blanket amnesty surely lies deeply and justifiably within the consciousness of many other people who have been treated with appalling degrees of cruelty and perversity. In the United States, both African Americans and Native Americans would have reasons to bear scars of unforgiven atrocities against their forbears. Hatreds have often subsided, replaced by cordiality and decency, but forgiveness might be too much to concede if it meant sacrificing a personal right to protest injustices that have never been confessed. Over time, the one domain the oppressed could call their own consisted of inner thoughts and feelings. They belonged inviolably to the abused, who as a consequence kept the abuser from holding exclusive rights to their common history and its interpretation.

For anyone in the grip of grim memories punctuated by bitterness and despair, resentment can be satisfying in a paradoxical sense. It may be a temporary defense, it may be self-defeating,

> "If I owe Smith ten dollars and God forgives me, that doesn't pay Smith."
> —Robert Ingersoll

it may be a false show of pride, and it may go against all the advice of the forgiveness scholars. But for all the supposed drawbacks and the likelihood that it will provide no permanent solution, it can give a victim a sense of power with which to hold the wrong in abeyance. It simply feels good until or unless something better comes along. Were it not so, why would it so often be seized upon as the reaction of choice? If unforgiveness is an instinct for self-preservation, then it is an asset that, like any other instinct, can also become destructive if carried too far.

The key factor in determining whether unforgiveness no longer serves its purpose is most commonly believed to be the passage of time. Virtually everyone who thinks about it expects those who have suffered hurts by others to react with rage and feelings of vengeance. By the same thinking, there can be no recovery without that angry turmoil. To gain our footing, in other words, we need to indulge our fury. How long it lasts and whether it ever basically changes is impossible to forecast with any certainty.

RESPECTING THE COMPLEXITIES OF TIME AND MEMORY

Take the example of Rose Foti, the woman in the Doblmeier film whose son, a New York City firefighter, was killed in the 9/11 attacks. She is visibly angry at the criminals who caused the disaster and the American authorities who allowed the pulverized piles of remains to be removed to a Staten Island land fill with the grimly ironic name "Fresh Kills" (from the Dutch word for "kil," a flowing stream of water). By moving the debris, authorities deprived her of the chance to find his fragmented remains. Later, we discover that she had been estranged from her son over his decision to remarry. He had gone against her wishes and her convictions. She explains that she refused to go to the wedding and implies that she judged his behavior unforgivable. Her love for him and grief over his death are deeply moving. At the same time, though she is sorry for the rift and regrets that the opportunity to reconcile with him is now gone, her words don't suggest a change of heart about the cause. In a poignant segment, she recounts the origin of the rupture when her son told her if she didn't attend the wedding, "I'm never going to speak to you again." Her reply, as she recalled, was, "So be it," adding that she hadn't been sorry for not attending. "And it strained our relationship in the last years of his life." Would she have sought forgiveness? She says wistfully, "You can't go back and ask forgiveness. He's gone," leaving open whether she would actually have done so.

Thousands of Catholics and their families have undergone torment of a different kind as the result of abuse of children by priests. In a scandal that spans decades and continues to produce victims, scores of priests have been formally accused of violating young people under their care. The dismay and outcry among large numbers of Catholic lay people have been enormous, and the collateral damage to the Church immeasurable. Priest abusers have been jailed, and some church leaders who were implicated in the cover-up of these crimes have been censured and disgraced. Cardinal Bernard Law was forced out as archbishop of Boston as a result. The entire Catholic Church in the United States was thrown into the gravest moral crisis in its history.

A state of tension persists as the Church attempts to repair the damage. Among those directly injured and those who identify with their cause, distrust and an unwilling-ness to forgive have become widespread. It is not the kind of charge that is eas-ily put aside, because it has

The loss of Rose Foti's firefighter son in the 9/11 attack has stirred mixed feelings in her.

victimized the most vulnerable members of the community and involved the collusion and conspiracy of the ordained clergy to keep its secrets. The survivors' groups want justice and have attained some of that, but they generally don't even mention forgiveness. Somehow a refusal to pardon guilty priests provides a balance to years of having forgiven them too much. It is a moral language everyone instinc-tively grasps. For most lawyers fighting for huge cash settlements, forgiveness is unthinkable, even laughable.

Somewhere along the line, someone is sure to introduce the "forgive but don't forget" strategy. This has become the middle ground between unforgiveness and a no-questions-asked pardon. By adopting it, the victim theoretically forgives the wrongdoer, thereby cleansing the feelings of rage and vengeance, but retains a mental account of the offense

as a form of self-protection. It is a neat and promising remedy if, in fact, if we can sort out the functions that easily. Experience tells me that it's unlikely that either one can be totally expunged short of a psychiatric malady of some sort. We can also use the non-forgetting part to assure those we purport to forgive that we are no pushovers. In fact, that may be the purpose of remembering, so we won't be caught off guard again.

The line between the one and the other is, however, rather permeable. A moment of "just remembering" can turn into a moment of "relived blame and resentment" at the slightest provocation. If a former friend swindles me out of $10,000 and eventually I forgive him, I might lapse back into those hard feelings the moment I see that he has won the lottery. Rather than distinct categories, forgive and forget seem fluid, unstable qualities that flow back and forth, at one time more detached and forgiving, at other times more forgetful, but rarely both at once.

Adultery and its aftermath offer an example. One partner to the marriage has engaged in infidelity. The other person uncovers the behavior and responds with hurt, anger, and a vow never to forgive. Time passes. The adulterer begs for forgiveness and makes good-faith efforts to assure the partner that it will never happen again. Action follows words as the adulterer pays more attention to his partner's needs and demonstrates a willingness to accept more responsibility for household chores, budgeting, and planning time together. The children, having felt the chill in the air, discover the root of the problem and urge the parents to seek counseling. The parents do. Over the course of many sessions, the unforgiver displays less anger but appears no more forgiving. The feeling of betrayal has become the principal weapon of defense against powerlessness. The infidelity conveys rejection and humiliation, leaving the offended one feeling both unjustly treated and worthless. Unforgiving rushes into the crisis with two at-least temporary fixes: to restore self-worth and to plant the flag for justice.

One day the logjam breaks. The offended party says it is possible to release the pain and suffering and fury that had churned inside. The explanation goes something like this: sufficient trust has been restored to go on; the greater good of the family is a key motive; life may never be the same between them but they can build anew; they share a love whose largesse can overcome betrayal. "I forgive you," the offended one says, "but at the same time I cannot be expected to forget."

Remembering, of course, makes stability hard to retain. If the offended one lets go of the grievance, the slate would apparently be wiped clean. Then suppose something suspicious happens. The former offender comes home late three nights in a row. Even if the reason for the lateness has nothing to do with infidelity, the circumstances cause the partner to wonder, then, perhaps to remember. Memory can then re-open the sluiceway between the unforgetting and the unforgiving. So long as the offense is lodged in the memory bank, it can be summoned by any number of particular associations. How could a sound mind not forget? Forgiving, unforgiving, and forgetting strike me as analogous to the states of matter—elements having the dynamic capacity to change from liquid, to solid, to gas and back again. Could that be a trinity of forgiveness?

Among Jesus' seven last "words" recorded in the Bible, one speaks directly about his persecutors: "Father forgive them, for they know not what they do." He offers that gift of grace without conditions. We might imagine someone else, left to die by a cruel army, saying rather, "Father, don't be in any hurry to forgive them, because they know perfectly well what they've done." And still another might draw on that urgency to say, "Father forgive them, but don't forget they're capable of such a thing."

The Unpredictable Calendar of Grace

Sister Helen Prejean, whose book *Dead Man Walking* and the movie based on it shed a powerful spotlight on capital punishment, takes a sympathetic stand toward unforgiveness as an authentic stage toward a replacement of hate with love. She spoke in an interview for the Doblmeier film within the context of her ministry within prisons, where the violent deeds and mental torture of convicted murderers intersect with the victims' families' vindictiveness and demands for retribution.

In an interview for the Doblmeier film, she stresses that either option must be authentic. "So it's not a 'should' placed on anyone: you should forgive. This is what's expected of you. The language of 'not an option' would make you think that. But it's an unfolding of the person in grace, where you reach a certain wholeness. And it has to do with love, that love will not be overcome.

"In a number of families I know, they go through the loss, the trauma, the grieving, the confusion feeling. Almost everybody begins pretend that you do." He added: "It may take a lifetime to reach different stages of forgiveness and at the same time you're going to have a lot of anger and resentment. So I don't think we should think about these things simplistically."

Moore and others reinforce the possibility that the un-forgiver's stand can be a rightful one. Rather than branding it a "bad" choice, it

---

"Forgiveness is the fragrance that the violet sheds on the heel that has crushed it."
—Mark Twain

---

is seen as a stressful place with its own moral underpinnings, whose goals are a measure of self-respect and balance of power. If it promises more than it can deliver, it still delivers something worthwhile in the absence of a better way.

For models of this stance, look no further than the Creator and the Creation.

UNFORGIVENESS: THE PERSISTENCE OF A SHADOW

God as creator of the universe is "good" in the eyes of the major faiths, yet in many strands of the tradition that goodness accommodates damning Satan and Satan's followers. The account of the final judgment in the Gospel of Matthew, alluded to earlier, condemns the goats to burn "in the eternal fire prepared for the devil and all his angels," whereas the sheep inherit the kingdom of heaven. Likewise, the expulsion of the devil & co. has been determined already in Genesis when the serpent, a symbol of the underworld figure, is thrown out of the Garden of Eden for tempting Adam and Eve to break their vow to God. In another story in the Hebrew Bible, the devil, known as the head angel, also enters into a friendly wager with God over Job's loyalty. The devil afflicts the godly Job with a series of horrible disasters in the hope that Job's faith in God will be shattered. It doesn't work, but the devil's true nature as the anti-God is confirmed.

In these biblical references to the devil, there isn't the slightest hint that God intends to extend an olive branch to his nemesis. The devil's works are presumed so extensive and so hideous as to rule out mercy. The final judgment appears to be final at least with reference to the "evil one" and the rest of the fallen angels. The religious traditions glorify God as a loving, forgiving Creator, but the devil, bad angels, and the goats lie outside the scope of this divine mercy. Sometimes an archangel can go too far.

Shakespeare might be excused for missing an exception to his observation that "the quality of mercy is not strained." The devil apparently strained God's mercy.

The creation likewise has an unforgiving side. I speak of the earth's silent protest against human efforts to exploit it. As the world's enterprises poison it, destroy its species, deform its natural beauties, disrupt its cycles, and twists its purposes, the earth bears the damage without offering the wrongdoers anything but their own self-inflicted punishment. The earth is unforgiving to those who abuse it without limit. Of the two creation accounts in Genesis, the one that emphasizes domination and exploitation has far overshadowed the one that captures a much greater sense of cooperation between humans and the earth. The second story, from the source known as the Yahwist, promotes more interdependence and balance, conjuring up a climate in which humankind and nature could be mutually forgiving. In the course of Western culture, however, the primary relationship has been a function of the first story's license to "subdue" the earth to the desires of peoples' perceived needs. The scientific and industrial revolutions accelerated this process by distancing and objectifying nature.

In our present crisis, nature is being diminished and cannot replenish or renew itself to keep up with the losses. It cannot rush in to make up for the errors and the wantonness of the ravagers. It is passively unforgiving and the consequences are, of course, potentially catastrophic.

The boundaries of forgiveness, then, are evident at the farthest reaches of the created order and within the nature of the Creator. Perhaps this means that there is a gap in all of us that remains essentially unbridgeable, a part of us that we cannot mend because it is a feature of our mortality to be without some degree of reconciliation. To be unforgiving almost seems inevitable, even natural, within a part of us.

The Complexity of Forgiveness

An Interview with
Thomas Moore

Psychotherapist Thomas Moore is a theologian who came to national prominence in 1993 with his widely acclaimed book Care of the Soul: A Guide for Cultivating Depth and Sacredness in Everyday Life. *A popular speaker, worship leader, and writer, he has continued to write works of spiritual guidance and wisdom, including* Soul Mates *(1994),* Original Self *(2001), and* Dark Nights of the Soul *(2005).*

I think that forgiveness is often romanticized. Even when you use the word, it's a little too precious. It's kind of wrapped in clouds—pink clouds. Sometimes it just seems unreal, and it can be experienced in that way, where it doesn't have much body to it, no guts behind it. On the other hand, at the same time, I do believe that if the community or an individual has really deeply developed their spiritual life, they will immediately forgive, and they can do it—and they can do it in such a way that doesn't mean that they don't also grieve. The Amish—at least the people I saw—seemed to be grieving as well as forgiving. I would say, though, that the best kind of forgiveness comes at the same time that you grieve—not only grieve but maybe resent, and maybe even hate. I don't think they are incompatible. In fact, if you could forgive, even though those feelings are there, it almost gives the forgiveness some bite and substance that it wouldn't have otherwise.

ANGER AND FORGIVENESS

During my life I've been betrayed a few times by friends and by people very close to me. You think a friend is going to be there for you, and they're not. Or you find out that they've really been saying some bad things about you but not to your face, and that sort of thing. It's funny, and it's really hard to sort out, but my own experience is that in some ways I feel I'm too quick to forgive.

I'm too quick to do it. I can quickly forgive somebody for almost any offense. And that forgiveness lasts about six months or a year, and then my resentment starts coming out. So I've learned about myself that I'm very quick to forgive. I know a lot of people who aren't, but I am very quick to forgive. But it doesn't go very deep, and I know that months or years from now I'm going to have to deal with those feelings.

I'll give you an example: a friend of mine who just died a few years ago was the chairperson of the department where I was teaching at a university, and they fired me, essentially. They didn't give me tenure at this university. And I had thought my whole life was going to be one of a college professor. That's all I thought about. So I didn't know where I was. And all my friends said, "What a rotten person that was. We thought this chairperson was your good friend, and he fired you." And I thought, "I should feel bad about this and angry. But I don't. What's wrong with me that I don't feel the anger? I'm not upset. That's who I am." And I would see him, and our friendship was very close, and it didn't bother me. But I realized over the years—that's about twenty years ago—I still feel some resentment for being fired. I still feel it. But at the same time in relation to my friend that forgiveness was immediate and it lasted.

What I'm saying is forgiveness is complex. Maybe on level *A* you forgive; on level *B* there's still some resentment going on; on level *C* you don't know what's going to come next. It's a complicated business, so I wouldn't expect it to be pure gold, your forgiveness. Another thing I feel strongly about as a therapist is that it's a good idea to realize that we have a lot going on with us at one time. It's very possible that forgiveness is developing in you just as resentment is also still there. It doesn't seem to be going away, and the anger—or whatever it is—is still there. So I don't think you can say, "Okay, here I am now suddenly today, I've begun forgiving this person. Now the anger's gone." It may take a lifetime to reach different stages of forgiveness and at the same time you're going to have a lot of anger and resentment. So I don't think we should think about these things simplistically.

PASSIONATE COMPLEXITY

I don't think you have to separate the hatred you might feel from forgiveness. They can be together. You can still hate, you can still feel terrible, you can still be grieving and at the same time forgive. That's my point. A human being usually has more than one thing going on at the same time. And it's the complexity that kind of drives them crazy. But I think if we can get it in our heads that we are complex in that way, and that it's okay to have a multitude of feelings, and to allow them to be very strong at the same time, that's fine.

When they hear me talk this way, people say, "Oh, you're talking about balancing your emotions." And I always say, "No I'm not talking about balance." I don't think this is some kind of highly spiritual—in that sense, intellectual—place where you say, "Oh, I can balance all these feelings out." No, you're going to feel your hatred passionately. You're going to feel your resentments passionately. You're going to feel your grief tremendously. And at the same time have the capacity to forgive. So I don't think it's a matter of balancing all those things out, it's being able to hold all of it at the same time. It's the bigness of the person that is at stake. Are you big enough to be able to hold all of these emotions at the same time? If you are, that's pretty good.

So I think we overdo forgiveness. We think, oh, we've got to forgive, and it becomes such a central thing. It's really a piece of a much more complicated quilt of emotions. So it's only one little piece of it. It's an important piece, but if it's separated from the rest of it I think we start talking about forgiveness in very odd ways that to me don't have much substance to them.

A DUTY NOT TO FORGIVE?

The shadow of forgiveness—the shadow of this whole business we're talking about—is that it's important not to forgive, also. If you don't feel that forgiveness, it's really important to protect that feeling of unforgiving. The unforgiving is as important as forgiveness. And you may have to hold that. There may be something very important in your incapacity to forgive, so don't run over it quickly. Don't let anyone talk you out of it. That's an important emotion to have too, and it's not because that's a step towards forgiveness. That's too easy. You don't know what's going to happen. You may spend your whole life not being able to forgive somebody. I think it's very important to be in that place. I don't think we should make a crusade of telling everybody that they should find forgiveness. I don't think that's a good place to be. It becomes one more moralism. Forgiveness is a gift, and if you don't have it don't pretend that you do.

Inexcusable? Yes, but not exactly unprovoked. It wasn't the fault of the cast-off brother that father loved him best, irritating as that was. But he had chosen to rub salt into that wound by informing them that the fates had already determined that he would be their boss for life and that the sun, moon, and stars would worship him. It's a boast we've all heard in one form or another. In this case, maybe it was all innocence on his part and maybe not. Even in the most well-adjusted families, however, those kinds of claims along with golden boy status are not likely to sit well, and they sure didn't with the brothers. Not surprisingly, perhaps, though not justifiably, they despised Mr. Big Shot and plotted how to dispose of him. Or so they thought.

This is the saga of Joseph, of course, and the Bible's account in Genesis throbs with raw, emotional nerve endings. Jacob, the patriarch, writhes in anguish at the apparent loss of his favorite son. The other 11 boys bury their guilt. The famine hits and the boys dash to Egypt looking for food. What they aren't prepared for is a shock. Joseph has survived and has become the chief of staff to Pharaoh. His duties include,

> "I am your brother, Joseph, whom you sold into Egypt. And now do not be distressed, or angry with yourselves, because you sold me here; for God sent me before you to preserve life."

lo and behold, dispersing emergency food supplies. He recognizes his conniving siblings right away, but his identity remains a mystery to them, perhaps owing to perks of his job, such as the fine cut of his toga and his use of top-notch Egyptian makeover treatments. He toys with them for a while, making them jump through hoops before giving them what they want. For example, he coerces them to go home and return with their youngest brother, Benjamin. As leverage, Joseph holds one brother hostage while the others are gone. Finally, the moment of truth arrives. Joseph gathers his brothers together and reveals himself to them, bursting into tears. The brothers are understandably dumbstruck.

"So Joseph said to his brothers, 'Come near to me, I pray you.' And they came near. And he said, 'I am your brother, Joseph, whom you sold into Egypt. And now do not be distressed, or angry with yourselves, because you sold me here; for God sent me before you to preserve life.'" Then the Bible says, "He kissed all his brothers and wept upon them; and after that his brothers talked with him."

Whether Biblical or Quotidian, a Transformative Force

The power of that moment is scarcely more imaginable than the spirit that prompted it. Its scope and beauty open to eternity. The gates of estrangement and sorrow and hurt break the lock of resistance to allow the mystery of love to overflow those who have been sequestered in guilt and shame. It didn't have to happen, but it did in such a way as to make the whole earth rejoice. The outcome least expected has emerged out of the heights and the depths of the unknown universe. Joseph kisses the brothers who plotted to rid themselves of him, and in that one instant recrimination evaporates.

The enactment of forgiveness can be incandescent.

Not all forgiveness reaches such dimensions, of course. Only sometimes does the drama shake the foundations of the earth. But whether it takes place on the level of grand opera or on the scale of a quiet end to a long, hard journey, forgiveness lifts a curtain on hope and possibility only barely envi-

> "Forgiveness is the remission of sins. For it is by this that what has been lost, and was found, is saved from being lost again."
> —St. Augustine

sioned beforehand. For no matter how much we anticipate some good coming out of an authentic act of forgiveness, the end is so much more than we imagined that we marvel over it.

Forgiveness' power cannot be reduced to a single feeling. Among the emotions it can evoke are love, generosity, relief, joy, release, triumph, and sorrow. It is a mixture of many, the sole province of none. At its most sublime, forgiveness brims with the power that is particular to any of those feelings, yet it is greater than the sum of those parts. Those who are fortunate enough to experience its various expressions testify to its ability to bring healing to a wide assortment of human afflictions of body, mind, and soul. A man I know who forgave his mother for abandoning him nearly 30 years earlier gained the freedom that allowed him to begin a new life. A woman I know embraced the vocation she had always longed for only after forgiving her former husband for humiliating her over many years. The occasions that initiate this miraculous process normally take place in private, but the effects become the stuff of a changed public persona.

The cures are not only many but often spectacular.

grain by telling her that he doesn't condemn her but forgives her, adding that she should "go and sin no more." Their brief interaction, in which the woman recognizes him as the Messiah, only hints at the rejoicing that must have swelled her heart and overflowed to those near to her.

If, as the Bible says, faith as tiny as a mustard seed can move mountains, can forgiveness do anything less? The source of forgiveness may be godly or an aspect of human potential. But whatever it is determined to be, it radiates inward to heal emotional ruptures and outward to stir onlookers to heights of freedom and truth they have never known before. It has the capacity to move and shake. If it is authentic, that is.

FOR SOME, REDRESSING POWER IMBALANCES MUST COME FIRST

A question arises. If forgiveness yields enormous power, can only those who are powerful do the forgiving? Could Joseph have forgiven the perfidy of his brothers if he had been a beggar in the streets of Egypt rather than a lofty figure in the royal court? Does the possession of earthly power itself—money, status, or authority—permit a granting of mercy and compassion that others couldn't justify? Must the meek inherit the earth before they can forgive those who abused them during their meekness?

Fred Keene is among those who believe something close to that. Keene's profession is mathematics, but he doubles as a biblical scholar whose special focus is the theology of the Scriptures. His particular concern about the relationship between power and forgiveness stems from the sexual violation of his wife by an Episcopal priest during her teens. He found many examples of clergy who tell such victims that the Bible expects them to forgive their abusers. Keene searched the Scriptures and came away with a starkly contrary conclusion: the Bible nowhere asks victims who are in the weaker position to forgive the stronger abusers. He rejects the idea that the Bible suggests otherwise, no matter what some Christians might say.

"The virtue of 'forgiving those who harm us' is part of Christianity's pervasive legacy to Western culture," Keene writes in an article, "The Politics of Forgiveness: How the Christian Church Guilt-Trips Survivors." "It is invariably attributed to the teachings of Jesus as found in the Christian Bible. Ironically, though, there is absolutely no scriptural basis for this notion of interpersonal forgiveness."

He continues, "What the New Testament does say is that people with more power should forgive people with less power—or, as in the case of first-century Christian communities, people should forgive each other because they are social equals ('brothers and sisters'). Nowhere in the Christian Bible is forgiveness even discussed, much less required, when the person who is harmed is less powerful than the person doing the harming."

In practice, however, Keene believes the victims at the lowest levels of society have usually been coerced to do the forgiving. He sees the purpose of this effort as protecting the status and reputation of the powerful. By forgiving their social superiors of the harm done to them, the weaker complainants not only cancel the debts of the privileged but also pardon their wrongs. The weaker classes are presumably told they have done their civic duty. The net result is to perpetuate a system in which the powerful can gain absolution from the damage they inflict. When, on the other hand, the powerful offer forgiveness, they might risk very little while gaining much public respect.

From his perspective on the ties between sexual abuse and religion, Keene believes that true forgiveness cannot occur unless power differences are resolved. Husbands and male clergy violate women who cannot or will not put up a fight against a greater force. Keene's prerequisites for making forgiveness possible include bringing about equality within troubled marriages and stripping clergy of the source of their privilege: their ordination.

Keene and others who encounter the results of sexual abuse have provided valuable insights into the situation in which abused people have often languished, misunderstood and isolated. They are most likely to come from the classes of people with less power. Think of the reign of lynching that terrorized African Americans well into the twentieth century. Or the poor kept in misery by miserly wages. Or women kept out of colleges and in the service of the egos of men who set the parameters of their lives. Or Native Americans seeing the fabric of their heritage rot within the preserves set aside to render them impotent. Eventually, I would guess, even the apparent boom of reservation casinos will be found to be in violation of one thing or another and cunningly curbed by outsiders who sense a loss of their control.

No wonder that forgiveness is so commonly identified with weakness. In everyday

> The victims at the lowest levels of society have usually been coerced to do the forgiving.

affairs, those who give it may be labeled wimps and gluttons for punishment. The strong never show such chinks in their armor, we are often told, because it would give an advantage to the other, often a competitor. Rather than display magnanimity, forgiveness demonstrates our inferiority. In the animal kingdom, we see what appears to be validation of this behavior. The weaker ones learn to bow and scrape in deference to the more powerful ones. Puppies learn this quickly or show the scars from trying to beat the system. For animals, however,

---

"People find it easier to forgive others for being wrong than for being right."
—J. K. Rowling

---

the order of things is a matter of survival, not the result of negotiating over wrongs that have been committed. Animals keep their hunkering to essential matters.

WHEN OUR MOTIVES AREN'T SO NOBLE AFTER ALL

For humans, of course, ending up in someone's good graces is much more involved. But humans retain the use of forgiveness as a survival tactic, sometimes for the better, usually for the worse. For example, the husband or wife who is petrified at losing a marriage may take personal blame for the wrongs committed by the other or make excuses for those wrongs that convey false pardon on them. This gives the weaker party a temporary reprieve from the dire consequences of the destructive path they are on. For the moment it softens the anger of the damaged, masochistic partner and gives the tormentor a degree of exoneration. It is manipulation for survival but goes much further to destroy the soul.

People with sadistic tendencies in relationships and societies use a pretense of forgiveness to exert more covert and calculated control over others. Former neighbors of mine illustrate the point. They were a close family of two parents and three children. The eldest child, a daughter, went off to college and used a credit card to rack up thousands of dollars in debt for trips, clothes, and luxury items. The parents were understandably frightened and outraged. After the initial outrage had somewhat subsided, the daughter and parents huddled together and agreed on a plan for paying off the bill (she would continue at school without a credit card and obtain a 25-hour-a-week job).

The parents were still shaken and leery, but before the semester had ended they told their daughter they had forgiven her but added a vow not to forget. They didn't forget; nor perhaps did they forgive. From then on, the parents cited that painful experience as a reason to monitor practically everything their daughter did, whether or not it involved the use of money or not. The hardship and embarrassment they had suffered were reasons for heightened vigilance and pragmatic safeguards. But the parents' trust in her had apparently been so shattered that they felt it necessary to intrude into her life as they never had before. Although they had forgiven their daughter with sincerity, their actions indicated that they had largely revoked forgiveness, using the age-old weapon of barely concealed anger as leverage to control much of her life.

Similar, more blatant deceptions enter into political relations among people. The United States government issued a variety of pardons and amnesties to Native Americans, only to attack tribes that took these sentiments seriously by laying down their arms. Likewise, the Trojan Horse seemed like a sure enough sign of forgiveness that the embattled city of Troy welcomed it inside its gates. Having lulled their foes into false security, the Greeks erupted from the horse and launched their devastating attack.

Genuine forgiveness can mingle with crass opportunism. Couples manifest this ambivalence in a particular fashion, especially in situations of infidelity. The one who is wronged, the presumed weaker partner, can acquire considerable power over the adulterer by forgiving him or her. It may be an earnest expression of the desire to let go of the anger and hurt while at the same time an opportunity to use some of that distress as emotional leverage with which to control the partner through guilt. We may all know a couple who has pursued those aims simultaneously, forgiving and, in effect, holding the other person hostage. The life went out of one marriage with which I'm familiar at the very time that forgiveness was extended to the faithless partner. Tranquility of a sort was restored, but the unfaithful partner, deeply remorseful, went to such lengths to avoid the risk of stirring up his partner's anger that spontaneity faded from their relationship.

Forgiveness power, therefore, can be as subtle and elusive as it is sometimes grand and far-reaching. But does it deserve its popular image as the behavior of the weak, an obsequious form of behavior that signifies an urge to survive?

Weakness, Strength, and the Moral Challenge of Pacifism

The first consideration is to ask what is meant by weak. By the world's standards, Jesus, Gandhi, Buddha, and Martin Luther King Jr., among others, were weak. They had no elite standing in society, they had no riches, they exhibited no desires to lead nations or conquer their enemies. They were all self-professed servants of something much larger than themselves. They weren't therefore powerful in the sense that the world implies, the ability to impose one's will on others through dint of financial, political, or military might. They did, however, bear within themselves the power of truth and wisdom. It gave them a quality of strength that went beyond the range of any other kind of strength. When they spoke, those around them heard wisdom that changed their lives without being forced or tricked or cajoled. These were "weak" teachers with powerful messages.

Jesus is represented in the New Testament as an ambiguous blend of earthly weakness and spiritual strength. On that basis, he would appear partly to challenge Keene's contention that the weaker person cannot justly forgive. He does forgive, to all intents and purposes,

as a weak, obscure figure. His godly authority, however, renders him as the strongest among the strong. Further, he does satisfy Keene's requirement that forgiveness require equality by approaching those he forgives as brothers and sisters.

Any disciple of Jesus or follower of other great religious traditions can exhibit a similar spiritual power. That would seem to qualify them as strong, no matter how humble or weak their social standing. An old adage says it's not the size of the dog in the fight; rather, the size of the fight in the dog. Something similar obtains here. No matter what the place of a believer in society, the intensity of that person's inner light matters infinitely more than theirs prestige or social power in infusing the power needed to forgive. The meek inherit the earth not because they are downtrodden but because they are spiritually blessed.

Therefore the question of who is weak and who is strong is often enigmatic. Less ambiguous, however, is that the presence of inner strength is indispensable, as we see in the paradoxes of Jesus' Meek & Co. Beatitudes. The motives behind the act of mercy count just as much. Only a strong, loving heart grounded in a transpersonal reality can bring about the power of forgiveness itself. "The weak can never forgive," Gandhi said. "Forgiveness is an attribute of the strong." Without this ineffable strength, the designs of the heart become contradictory, even demonic.

In its purest form, mercy is given freely without expectations. Don Kraybill, the Elizabethtown College professor, highlighted one historic instance of that purity, the sixteenth-century martyrdom of a Dutchman named Dirk Wilheims.

"He was in prison for his faith and scheduled to be executed," Kraybill began. "But he escaped from prison. It was winter and he was running across the ice of a pond. He turned back and saw the jailer following him, and Dirk made it across safely. But the jailer fell into the water half way across the lake. Dirk returns, rescues the jailer, pulls him out, saves him. And when they get back on dry ground, the jailer recaptures him, takes him back to the prison and two or three days later he is killed as a martyr."

Kraybill's conclusion reflects on the recent actions by the Amish toward the family of the man who killed their children: "This is a story of love for the enemy, and forgiveness for the enemy, and that is an image that is in the Amish mind today of what is expected in Christian duty in terms of how you respond to enemies or how you respond in forgiveness to those who are evil to you and those who inflict violence on you."

Nowhere are the paradoxes of weak and strong more evident than when weighing the morality of pacifism and nonviolent resistance. The mere mention of pacifism stirs strong emotions and sharp debate. Many believe that peaceful opposition to physical force is a noble ideal, even though they reject it as an option for themselves. Others consider it a well-meant but fuzzyheaded recipe for destruction. Those in the middle feel the pull of its moral

---

Nowhere are the paradoxes of weak and strong more evident than when weighing the morality of pacifism and nonviolent resistance. The mere mention of pacifism stirs strong emotions and sharp debate.

---

appeal and would use it as a strategy on selective occasions but couldn't adopt it as a total lifestyle.

How does pacifism relate to forgiveness? Are they the same thing? The short answer for me is that pacifism acts out the meaning of forgiveness by forsaking vengeance and hostility in the face of evil that is both evident and potential. Nonviolent resisters dedicate themselves to giving up the urges and thoughts of retaliation and to loving their enemies by refusing to fight them. The pacifists themselves may be victims, or they may align themselves with victims of war and violence. That is, they may have personally borne the slings and arrows of aggression, or they may be standing ready to bolster the cause of those who are under attack. The pacifist's willingness to let go of anger and resentment and to offer the aggressor a gift of peace goes to the heart of the forgiveness truth and power. In declining to retaliate, the non-resister, like every forgiver, extends a hand of life and love to one who has caused harm or intends to.

The exercise of nonviolence implies that physical violence is being used or threatened and therefore represents a particular kind of offense. If an army attacks an innocent village or a mugger beats up a random pedestrian, the nature of the wrong is clear. But the actions that call for forgiveness obviously extend to circumstances that don't involve physical force. Slander, financial fraud, and betrayal are some of the offenses that normally don't entail physical force. Therefore, physical violence covers only a portion of the situations that would invite forgiveness.

The nonviolent response to assault, however, is either a high calling or a rejection of personal responsibility, depending on one's basis for judgment. To the pacifist, absorbing the blows or threats of bodily harm fulfills a mandate to side with the force of peace, the highest good. To the nonpacifist, such a strategy may be worse than foolhardy or naïve. It can be seen as a refusal to pursue justice as a prerequisite to considering any kind of forgiveness. For the nonpacifist, a physical defense is necessary to deter the aggressor and to spare potential victims pain and suffering. It is part of the thinking behind "just-war" theory in Christian tradition that permits the use of violence under certain criteria. While the pacifist's nonretaliation, therefore, is a unilateral, free, and internally self-contained choice that includes no pre-conditions, the nonpacifist cannot as a rule even consider forgiveness until the physical well-being of the victim or potential victim has been defended.

NONVIOLENT COMMUNITY: "WITH THE GRAIN OF THE UNIVERSE"

During the civil rights era in America, two perspectives were starkly evident in the opposition between Dr. King's nonviolent resistance movement and the black power advocacy of Stokley Carmichael, Malcolm X, H. Rap Brown, and others. The dispute between the two sides was grounded essentially in differences over how to discharge the rage that had built over generations of abuse of blacks by whites. In the short term, at least, King's pacifism had the greater influence over public opinion. As an admirer of Mahatma Gandhi's nonviolent resistant tactics, King defused many Americans who might have sanctioned the use of lethal force to put down a militant crusade by civil rights advocates.

King's cause and Gandhi's success in ousting the British from India stand as the two great models of pacifism in the twentieth century and gave it wide credibility as a power unto itself, even among many people who believed it to be too extreme for their use. With King and Gandhi achieving huge changes in attitudes and policy by sitting at lunch counters and marching in streets lined with haters, how could anyone dismiss the power of nonviolence in human affairs? Here were believers refusing to fight not only fire with fire but even fire with water. Implicit in this approach was forgiveness of a kind echoed in King's vow to love his enemies, no matter how much violence was visited upon them as victims.

King was indebted not only to the Hindu, Gandhi, but to the "peace churches" that have long kept a pacifist-forgiveness vigil for Christians. Biblical scholars and historians tell us that the first Christians were nonviolent in imitation of Jesus, but that tradition was largely forgotten when the church became a faith-based subsidiary of the Roman Empire, which needed religious arguments to prop up the rationale for its war machine. Hence, just war theory. Some wars are justified, St. Augustine said, if they observe certain rules like a "just cause," the use of reasonable force, and proper authorization. If these standards were all but impossible to satisfy individually, the task of fulfilling the collection of them was perhaps Sisyphean. Be that as it may, the Christian establishment has used that yardstick, more or less, to judge the worthiness of wars ever since. Only in the past decades has pacifism again been acknowledged as a valid teaching within Catholicism. Conscientious objection won favor in the Catholic Church and other churches.

Meanwhile, the peace churches kept the flame flickering for more than 400 years before the recent nonviolent campaigns captured the world's attention. The Amish, the Mennonites, the Brethren, the Quakers, and others that grew out of the Protestant Reformation had he says, "Nonviolence is cooperative, participatory power. It is relational—'power with' as opposed to 'power over.' It is a force in partnership with others as opposed to dominion over others."

Gingerich is centered in the lessons of the earthly Jesus. "We have a body of political science supporting the thesis that power is nonviolence. We have a rich set of historical movements, particularly within the past century, demonstrating 'a force more powerful' than violence. And as I have already begun to indicate, this understanding of power is rooted in the biblical heritage of the prophets and the example and teachings of Jesus."

Dr. King's ability to create a broad nonviolent civil rights coalition was largely possible because of his acceptance of both theistic and non-theistic interpretations of pacifism. Calling nonviolent resistance a "conviction that the universe is on the side of justice," he allowed in his book *A Testament of Hope* that there were "devout believers in nonviolence who find it difficult to believe in a personal God. But even these people believe in the existence of some creative force that works for universal wholeness. Whether we call it an unconscious process, an impersonal Brahman, or a Personal Being of matchless power and infinite love, there is

a creative force in this universe that works to bring the disconnected aspects of reality into a harmonious whole."

Pacifism played out on large stages of the world has made its indelible mark, yielding waves of forgiveness beyond measure or effect. These are the grand illustrations. But forgiveness power is indivisible. When it occurs, it permeates all the space around it, like beauty or love. Any setting in which it takes place fills the participant and the observer to overflowing. Hence it is most likely to exert its invisible force in the common transactions of the day.

As striking as the Amish reaching out to the family of their children's killer is the picture of the two men sitting side by side in a classroom in *The Power of Forgiveness*. Azim Khamisa is a Sufi Muslim of Iranian descent. Next to him is Ples Felix, a Southern Baptist and African American. Felix's grandson and guardian had murdered Khamisa's son in a dispute over a pizza. Khamisa observed the 40 days of Sufi mourning and sought out Felix to help him reach out to kids to stop the killing. It was, as Khamisa recalls, an action that invited the "higher plane" that we have within us. It was, of course, an act of forgiveness. Felix agreed. He is grateful, he says, in ways he and his family "cannot express," adding that it's "all so powerful, I can only tell

Azim Khamisa and Ples Felix.

you by extension it's something that we all want to experience at the point of really needing it."

The gentle words of the two men, talking to children they hope to reach with their message of nonviolence, are embodied in the calmness and comfort they exude. "The long term benefit of that forgiveness," Felix says, "is that Azim and I are brothers. He is my best friend. There is nothing I wouldn't do for Azim Khamisa; there's nothing that he wouldn't do for me."

From Condemnation to Compassion

An Interview with
Thich Nhat Hanh

Some of our closest relationships demand the most of us in the way of forgiveness and reconciliation. Here the venerable Buddhist monk and spiritual guide Thich Nhat Hanh reflects on what he learned as part of the Buddhist peace movement in Vietnam and on the long and patient process of dealing with hurt and offense from someone we know well—a spouse, a child, a close friend.

LESSONS FROM THE VIETNAM WAR

In Vietnam, there was a lot of suffering, and people became enemies of each other. In such a situation you have to find a way to survive and to help others survive. There was a peace movement trying to end the war, and many young people joined in. We had to show people the way to act properly, because if you do not have peace within yourself it is very difficult to work for peace. Peace in oneself, then peace in the world.

Our thinking was, man is not our enemy. Our real enemies are misunderstanding, discrimination, violence, hate, anger. And with that kind of insight we conducted the peace movement. North Vietnamese were fighting in the South, South Vietnamese were fighting back, American soldiers were fighting. We looked upon them as victims of policy that did not come out of a right understanding. When you see the other person as a victim, you don't get angry with him or her anymore. You try to deliver him or her from the kind of view, the kind of anger, the kind of confusion, that has made him or her like that.

So hate is not born from your heart. Instead there is a compassion. And you don't see that person as an enemy. You see that person as someone you would like to help. And you see that the real enemy is the confusion, the violence, the dissuasion that are there in the heart of the person. You try to remove that from him or from her. You have to learn and train yourself how to do that.

And that is really peace work. Peace work does not mean that you go down the street and shout against the government. Instead, we chanted, we composed songs. And there is a song that goes like this, "Man is not our enemy. If we kill man, with whom shall we live?"

If you are filled with anger in what you do, what you say, you create more suffering for yourself than for the other person. When you are inhabited by the energy of anger, you want to punish, you want to destroy. And that is why those who are wise do not want to say anything or do anything while anger is still in them. But the wise person will try to bring peace into himself or herself first. Then he or she will have a right view on the situation. When you are calm, when you are lucid, you'll see that the other person is a victim of confusion, of hate, or violence transmitted by society, by parents, by friends, by environment. And when you are able to see that, your anger is no longer there. You can look at him or her with compassion; and instead of trying to punish him or her, you try to help him or her out of that situation. This is the real practice of peace. Because we started the peace movement in Vietnam in the circle of Buddhist practitioners, we knew the spiritual dimension of peace.

RECONCILING PERSON TO PERSON

When you listen to the other person, you have to nourish the intention, the desire to help the other person to speak out. Maybe so far no one has been able to listen to him because he was very harsh in speaking. You have to be very compassionate in order not to get angry when you listen to him, because his speech may be full of condemnation and blame and judgment. And if you don't nourish compassion in yourself, you cannot listen very long. And even if his speech is full of wrong perceptions and blaming, you continue to listen. You say to yourself: "I am listening to him with only one purpose, to give him a chance to empty his heart. I am doing charity work. I'm doing compassionate work."

If you remember that during the whole time of listening, then compassion in you will protect you from anger. Otherwise anger will emerge. That is why compassion is the antidote to anger. With compassion you can relate to other people; without compassion you are cut off. That is why nourishing compassion is very important. Then you see that the other person has suffered, and he or she has not been able to take care of his own or her own suffering. They have inflicted a lot of suffering on themselves and the people around them. Instead of punishing him or her, you, who know the practice, try to help him or her by your practice of compassionate listening and loving speech.

THE LANGUAGE OF LOVING KINDNESS

You know very well that punishing will not help. Only compassion can help. That is why you are determined to practice compassion by just sitting there and listening to him and to her. "I know you have suffered a lot in the last many years. I know that. I'm sorry that I have not been able to help you. Instead of helping to make the situation worse by responding in anger to you, now I know that is wrong. I want to help you. I do not want to make you suffer. So, darling, please tell me what is in your heart. If I understand your suffering and difficulty, I will not make mistakes again and make you suffer again. Please help me. Tell me what is in your heart. If you don't help me, who will? So please tell me." That is the language of loving kindness.

When you listen with compassion, with all your heart, you listen in order to help him or her to empty his or her heart. You don't try to correct him or her right now. You have plenty of time to do that later on.

One hour of listening like that can relieve a lot of suffering out of the other person. And if you want to help him or her, you'll then find opportunities to help him or her remove wrong perceptions in him or her, because wrong perception is at the base of anger, desperation, hate, and violence. A few days later, when you have an opportunity, you can provide him or her with a little bit of information, so that he can use it in order to correct his perception. Just a little bit of information, the dose that he or she can accept. And then you help him or her to change his or her perceptions gradually. And when that person has got right perceptions, his anger, his suffering, his desire to punish will vanish. This takes a lot of courage, patience, and compassion to do; but many couples—like father and son, mother and daughter, husband and wife—have applied that and have been able to reconcile with each other. It works.

YOUR OWN GROWTH

It is because that person suffers, not because he has Buddha nature or has God in him, that you have to be nice to him. God does not need your compassion. The human being who suffers is the one who needs your compassion. You know very well that without compassion you cannot be happy. You are very alone. You are cut off from the world. Compassion makes happiness possible, and if you are not capable of being compassionate you are not capable of being happy. And that's why practicing compassion is not for his or her sake alone. It is for you.

What is the meaning of meditation or praying? The purpose of the practice is to understand, is to be aware of what is going on. And what is going on is that you suffer, and the other person suffers. That is the first noble truth in Buddhism: suffering is a reality. The practice begins with the awareness that suffering is there in you and in that other person. When you have seen suffering, you are motivated by the desire to remove suffering—the suffering in you and the suffering in him—because if he still suffers, it will make you suffer somehow later on.

So helping someone remove the suffering in himself means doing something for yourself also. Thus compassion is directed to yourself and to the other person at the same time. And the intention to remove suffering is there. But you need the concrete practice in order to do so. The intention is not enough. The intention to love is not love yet. If you don't know how to love, you make the loved one suffer more, like a father who tries to love his son but destroys his son by his love. That is why right love, true love is what you have to learn.

When you see the suffering of the other person, if you are motivated by the desire to help him or her, it means that you begin to have compassion in you. That is very good. And as you are able to help him or her to suffer less, to stop suffering, then you get joy. Happiness is made of that kind of joy. Happiness does not mean that you have the capacity to consume a lot. Happiness means that you feel that your life has meaning. You are able to help so many people.

Consider again a father and son alienated from each other. When the son becomes capable of practicing understanding and compassion, he no longer suffers. The father in him is also transformed, because the father is in the son. The son is a continuation of the father. So looking into the son deeply, you see the father. And if the son is transformed by understanding and compassion, the father in him also has a transformation. That is why it is very important to begin the practice within. Each has to work it out in himself first. When you are light, when you are protected with compassion and understanding, when you have already forgiven and you are free from anger, that is the moment when you can become very effective in helping to change the situation.

Five

Forgiving Oneself

You are "all jammed up," you say. That is, you're a psychological mess, a clogged emotional drain. It's been like that for a long time, but you think it's been getting worse. As near as you can tell, it's a case of feeling negative about yourself; a layer cake of bad feelings. Guilt is a big chunk of it for sure, but only part. There is plenty of regret and blame covered with a layer of fear. You're mad at yourself and practically everything else. It's as if a jury has convicted you and even the best lawyers couldn't reverse the verdict. Worst of all, you're usually the butt of your own jokes.

to the initiative by Azim Khamisa to ask the grandfather of his son's killer to start a foundation to prevent violence among young people. Compared to those relatively overt expressions, the signs of self-forgiveness are much more difficult to identify. It is a transaction within the personal soul whose traces can take a long time to spot, if ever. A number of years ago, I spoke with a well-known country singer about his many years of self-blame covered over with a variety of addictions. He had ended that destruction, and when I asked him what made that possible, he said he had forgiven himself. How did he know? I asked. "I don't hate any more," he replied.

At the crossroads, then, many sources of wisdom, insight, and enigma await you. The following is an attempt to winnow some of the thoughts and experiences that arise from the search for self-forgiveness that you may find helpful. It is by no means a comprehensive review of those voices because, in a real sense, the phenomenon is far from being comprehensible.

The Inner Tussle

Therapists are the most common advocates of forgiving ourselves, even though there is little agreement among them about its nature. Whatever it is, they seem united in believing that their patients often get much better if they can vault that big hurdle. The therapists sort out various benefits: it brings the self-hating client awareness that the "bad" he or she feels is just part of a much larger "good" self; it relieves the crushing burden of constantly rehearsing past sins; it breaks the stranglehold of self-centeredness that may be thought to accompany the obsession with one's wrongs; and many others. At the same time, the therapist-advocates in general don't try to explain what it is that's providing these benefits. Nor do they, as a rule, pretend to know exactly where the capacity to achieve such breakthroughs comes from.

The direction in which this discussion heads is largely dependent on what kinds of charges one has leveled against oneself, whether they are the "I'm just worthless" kind that float up from the ether of one's existence for barely discernible reasons, or the type that lodge in our consciousness from having gotten away with forging a batch of bank checks or from having slept with my husband's best friend.

Both kinds may weigh heavily, and both deserve attention in the view of many counselors. But the hard cases of actual wrongdoing incite the most passion about self-forgiveness, pro and con.

Skeptics, as you might expect, are wary of the process. They're suspicious of the rhetoric and routines of self-forgiveness. They don't dismiss the gains from any therapeutic practices, for whatever reasons, but question the underlying premises behind this particular emphasis. To the skeptic, the concept of self-forgiveness is a cop-out for the weasels, a game of psychological flimflam by which the scoundrel wriggles out of responsibility. And what about the victim? Isn't it grossly unfair to the person who was cheated blind at a work site when the perpetrator "forgives" him- or herself for doing so? To the doubters, it all sounds like moral evasion that adds the insult of pardoning oneself for the original injury.

According to the analyst, therefore, self-forgiveness is regarded either as progress or regression—a gateway to freedom from pain and remorse or a deceptive end-run around the truth. Motives have everything to do with it, and motives are nearly always mixed. For everyone who seeks forgiveness as a means of living more honestly and compassionately, there is surely another who wants to lift the yoke of sin in order to sin again. The dynamics can be so complex that they include both of those elements or more. Some suffering souls seek escape by creating a mental fantasy that elevates them above their guilt without actually erasing it. Others cling to a thin rope of hope that has mysteriously answered their prayers for relief from the misery of evil deeds, as the drowning grab hold of a tree branch. The inner tussle may pit the worthy ends of conscience against the survival instincts of rationalization and willpower. The desire to clear one's name in one's own thoughts can produce both fictions about the past and earnest pleas for healthy restoration.

Whatever becomes mixed up in the halting process of seeking forgiveness for oneself, the impulse to seek some kind of peace within a mind that is at war with itself appears to be universal. It is human to want to settle the conflicts between the forces of guilt, whether they are actual transgressions against another or simply feelings of worthlessness, and the forces of forgiveness. How the struggle turns out results from a host of factors like temperament, circumstances, and beliefs. Whether someone dives into this exercise and emerges renewed or deceived is beyond prediction or control. The phenomenon remains an enigma, but for all that is no less compelling and irresistible as a human striving.

Thomas Moore, the wise counselor and author, emphasizes that self-forgiveness is as uncontrollable as it is indispensable for mental and spiritual health. Forgiveness in general cannot be commanded or engineered, he says, but it is possible to prepare the way by becoming aware and humble. "The important thing," he says in the Doblmeier interview, "is not to be somebody special. But to be quite ordinary."

If we beat ourselves with the stick of perfectionism, we are sunk, Moore says. Religion may twist our minds into thinking we ought to be more virtuous than we have any right to expect of ourselves. As the result of that and other influences, the punishment imposed on the self by the self makes freedom seem utterly impossible. We've failed at marriage. We've failed at work. We are bad and that's that. To find that freedom, Moore says, it's crucial to "realize that we are like other people," neither better nor worse.

"We look at ourselves and say, 'I'm not so great, I'm just a human being and therefore I have to forgive myself constantly because I'm always going to be doing things that I wish I weren't doing. Or I may even do things that will hurt other people. I may not intend it, but it's happening. And so I have to forgive myself over and over again. I tell you from my point-of-view forgiveness is something that is constant. And maybe that would make it easier to forgive someone else,

*Author and therapist Thomas Moore (*Care of the Soul*) says that self-forgiveness often leads to an easier forgiveness of others.*

some other person. If you could realize that constantly you've got to forgive yourself."

The Gospel story of the tax agent and the Pharisee serves as a neon illustration. As the Gospel relates it, the two men entered the temple to pray. The Pharisee thanked God that he was "not like other men," like the lowly tax collector, but a fine fellow who obeyed the moral rules. By comparison, Jesus says, the browbeaten tax man begged mercy as if he were nothing special at all: "God, be merciful to me a sinner." In one of those marvels of spare utterance in the New Testament, Jesus applies the stunning tag line: "I tell you, this man [the tax collector] went down to his house justified rather than the other; for everyone who exalts himself will be humbled, but he who humbles himself will be exalted."

Moore is among those who believe that forgiveness is a function of self-love and that it requires "some kind of spiritual achievement within yourself" that is a mystery and may have nothing to do with organized religion. His minimalist definition is this: "I think it takes vision, it takes the capacity to transcend raw emotion, to be able to forgive. Further, in looking for forgiveness we have to reach so far beyond ourselves and beyond our human capacity and be open to the mystery of what it means to be

"Children begin by loving their parents; as they grow older they judge them; sometimes they forgive them."—Oscar Wilde

a person. . . . Yes, there's a sense in which forgiveness is divine."

SEEKING GUIDANCE IN THE MARKET OF THERAPY AND SELF-HELP

Problems that lead people to counseling usually stem from self-condemnation, Moore finds. "I practiced psychotherapy for 30 years," he notes, "and I think most of the problems that I've seen people struggle with have to do with this issue. If ever they could forgive themselves for something they may have done, something that has happened, and finally reached forgiveness for someone else, I think their emotional problems would ease at that very point. But that's a very difficult thing to achieve; it's not easy to reach the point where you can forgive yourself. If you can, well, almost anything is possible."

A friend hopes he is closer to crossing that divide but still holds back. Over time, he has taken hold of various religious traditions in

Author and lecturer Marianne Williamson says,"At a time when we see so much evil, we are called upon . . . to stand for the possibility of human redemption that turns even the hardest of hearts."

hopes of finding a god that would make sense to him. Most recently, he has embraced the concept that he belongs to an indivisible state of being that animates the universe. In other words, he is something of a Buddhist who subscribes to the view that he participates in a oneness that in no way sets him apart as special in Moore's sense (eliminates the concept of "self," in fact). Why is self-forgiveness, then, so elusive? "Because somehow I still believe I am unique." He can think that's

absurd, but stronger mental suppositions keep him hemmed in. Awarding forgiveness to the self—with or without divine help—might be similar to the process of forgiving another person who makes a confession and receives both a pardon and, perhaps, appropriate restitution. By this thinking, the self is a relatively objective entity. The self would need to search the sources of guilt and misery and confess them to the "victim" self. A thorough airing of the wrongs would transpire in this internal dialogue. At some point, the forgiving self would absolve the guilt-ridden self. But that could only happen if the exchange was open, honest, and thorough. Otherwise, it would count for naught.

To the outsider looking in, including that part of the forgiveness-seeking self that conducts an inventory of the darker side and interprets those findings, the difference between sincere and insincere motivations can be difficult to detect. Illusions and distortions pop up everywhere. Marianne Williamson, the well-known writer on peace and spirituality, offers this analogy as an antidote to fooling oneself. Referring to a "double bind" that leads us to an unbalanced view, she says in her interview for the film: "If you go to a therapist and your therapist only wants to talk to you about what you've done right, you're at the wrong therapist. If you go to your therapist and talk about the disasters in your life and your therapist doesn't want to take any look whatsoever—even the smallest part you might have played in attracting the disaster, no matter how heinous . . . you're at the wrong therapist."

In *The Self-Forgiveness Handbook: A Practical and Empowering Guide*, counselor and writer Thom Rutledge insists that seeking the truth is essential to gaining psychological health. "A common fear," he writes, "is that self-forgiving is a snazzy, politically correct, socially acceptable way of letting ourselves off the hook by avoiding accountability and personal responsibility. This is absolutely not true." He advises readers to wake up to their inner conflicts and, like Moore, to see themselves as victims of idealistic expectations they had been taught in their early years. Rutledge, whose other books include *Embracing Fear*, has attracted considerable attention and sees his mission as helping patients see themselves lovingly rather than cruelly.

Practitioners of rational or cognitive therapy have made significant inroads in promoting a sane and honest perspective. Advanced by the University of Pennsylvania and other psychiatric centers, this school was popularized by psychiatrist Dr. David Burns in his hugely best-selling book, *Feeling Good: The New Mood Therapy*. The book outlines a treatment for depression, a condition often identified with inability to forgive oneself. The cognitive therapists basically operate on the assumption that distorted or erroneous thoughts about oneself trigger malignant feelings such as "I'm no good" and other forms of self-hatred. Therefore, ridding a patient of irrational thoughts that have no basis in fact frees him or her from the penalties of holding fast to such opinions. (The street slogan goes, "If you don't like the way you're feeling, change the way you're thinking.") The goal isn't to evade the truth of one's behavior or experience but to weed the facts from the lunatic ideas and feelings that have crept into the soul of the patient without justification or in exaggerated form to plunge the patient into despair. Reason becomes the tool to separate reality from unreality without any obvious need for a spiritual enabler. That may produce self-forgiveness all by itself or become a vital first step.

The self-help enterprise arises at a time in our national life when the self has suffered a disaster from a paradox—battered simultaneously by the lure of the narcissistic spotlight and the terrors of anonymity and loneliness. The self-helpers respond, not surprisingly, in response to those causes, some dwelling on propping up the bruised ego of the depressed and forlorn, others pointing the budding achievers toward the kinds of "impossible dreams" whose goal is celebrity of one variety or another. Not all in the movement to shore up wounded selves contribute to the problem, of course. Some like Moore and Burns have translated complex and refined wisdom of the ages into language and practices suffering people

can use without having to pay for a therapist. This mass marketing of all sorts of techniques mingles scoundrels with saviors, a hodgepodge that needs to be sorted out. But I'm assuming this scattershot process on balance does both good and harm. You plunk down your money for the books or tapes or CDs and take your choice of gurus.

The tendency of self-help advocates to promise happy outcomes with willpower and positive thinking can undermine genuine self-forgiveness by encouraging people to manufacture a false self that defies reality. Over the decades, the American drive toward its own notions of success has created a huge market for preachers, doctors, professors, and others who provide coaching for those who strive to win, spelling out their own versions of the steps needed to win. The aim has been to mold personalities to send them into the competitive fray. That agenda by its very nature precludes looking at the traits in that competitive system that may cause and perpetuate the problems in the first place. Many self-help programs equip the self with the right tools and send it into a system that may be destroying it. At any rate, it is a designed self that resists self-fulfillment. Another marketing goal of self-help has been to serve the interests of the therapeutic network by playing the part of a "good" parent, extending total acceptance and applying a veneer of false optimism and self-justification to a bruised ego. It's music to the sufferer's ears and money in the therapist's banks. *I'm OK, You're OK*, or as the late prophetic voice of William Sloane Coffin put it: "I'm not okay, you're not okay, and that's okay."

Opportunists may be in the minority, but they have gained the lion's share of the attention because the rewards they offer most often are material gain and prestige. Many of them have landed on easy street themselves by allegedly pointing the way to easy street. A whiff of doubt always trails these promotions and cure-alls, however. It is the type of skepticism that follows financial advisers who promote riches to ordinary folks on television and in popular books.

Social Scientists Begin to Sketch the Terrain

Self-forgiveness has attracted surprisingly little interest from scholars. A recent article by two professors at the State University of New York at Buffalo summarized all academic writing on the subject, and their conclusion was underscored in the headline: "Self-Forgiveness: The Stepchild of Forgiveness Research." Professors Julie H. Hall and Frank D. Fincham note that overall studies of forgiveness have been rapidly increasing but that self-forgiveness has "received remarkably little attention in the burgeoning literature."

What do Professors Hall and Fincham find within these limited explorations? Self-forgiveness studies are a cluster of hypotheses without much supporting evidence so far. The lack of abundant proof doesn't make the theories any less intriguing, however. The forgiveness scholars show both the resolve and the curiosity to launch this neglected area of study into prominence. By coming to clear hypotheses, they have taken the first major step toward scientific results.

Hall and Fincham find a definition of self-forgiveness in their survey that matches what is offered by forgiveness scholarship in general: somehow all the guilt and anger against oneself needs to be converted to acceptance and compassion toward oneself. That is the road that must be traveled. The scholars would like to know what moves us along that road and what the consequences of getting there might be, but they don't claim much progress yet. The general view Hall and Fincham discern is that it usually takes quite a lot of time. One of the scholars

Forgiveness in Christian Perspective

An Interview with
Rev. James A. Forbes Jr.

A nationally prominent preacher in an historic pulpit, the Rev. James A. Forbes Jr. is Senior Minister Emeritus of the Riverside Church in New York City, where he served for eighteen years. Having also served as a professor of preaching at Union Theological Seminary for a dozen years, Rev. Forbes is currently President of the Healing of the Nations Foundation and host of "The Time Is Now" on Air America Radio.

A BETTER LIFE

The symbol of the cross cannot be dismissed when one comes to actually living one's life. Here is a man, Jesus, who did good, who went about healing and preaching and talking love. But now he's apprehended and brought up on trumped up charges. And what does he say, even when he's nailed to a cross? He says, "Father, forgive them. They know not what they do." Now that symbol either means something or it doesn't. So if anyone says, "I'm a Christian," it means that the founder of their faith lived a life in which he not only urged them to pray for forgiveness, but he also modeled forgiveness. So where does my calling to forgive come from? It comes from Jesus the Christ, who says in his teaching and his living that the quality of life God intended for us requires that we not get hung up, locked-into, held hostage to offenses that have come our way. We must find a way to throw it off on grace, to forgive people—not to spend your time either in revenge or, in regards to yourself, in perpetual regret. But you have to find a way to say to yourself, "Yes, offenses will come, but I'm too busy living out my life to hold offenses, so thank God for the religious instruction that says 'You know what? You live a better life when you practice forgiveness.'" That's the way it begins for me.

CHANNELS OF FORGIVENESS

The other issue is that the best way to begin to talk about forgiveness is not to tell folks to forgive their enemies. That's hard as the beginning point. First let them think about how much forgiveness God has had to grant them from their childhood to up to their level of maturation. They have had to make withdrawals from the Bank of Grace many, many times. So let's just help people to ask, "How much forgiveness have you needed in order to get up and go through your life without an inordinate fixation on the guilt and the shame of your past?" That's a good place to begin, because as the prayer says, "Forgive others, and if you don't forgive others neither will your heavenly Father forgive you." That's really the teaching mode. Really what it says is that people who are not willing to extend forgiveness will close off the channels of forgiveness when they need it. So blessed are the merciful for they shall obtain mercy.

Six

The Justice Factor

For a few days in April 2007, the brash radio celebrity, Don Imus, was in the national spotlight. In typical fashion, he had been using his rapier tongue to lacerate a victim for a few laughs and to inject his ego with another quick upper. Only this time, he fell on his own sword by denigrating the Rutgers University women's basketball team, calling them "nappy-headed hos." The incident sparked a firestorm of anger and demands that Imus be thrown off the air. For his part, Imus apologized repeatedly and tried to convince an attentive public that he wasn't a racist but was only trying to be funny. His employers at the National Broadcasting Company, which televised his show, and his nationwide radio carrier, the Columbia Broadcasting System, fired him in less than a week.

On the day of his ousting by CBS, Imus kept his agreement to meet with the Rutgers women's team at the New Jersey Governor's Mansion to offer his regrets formally. He did so, and shortly thereafter the women and their coach said they had accepted Imus's apology and were in the "process of forgiving" him. It was an extraordinarily generous response on the part of the college women. These college women had become the adults to Imus's child. Despite the cutting insult hurled at them—the racial and sexist implication of being caricatured as primitive and promiscuous—they had accepted his bid to tell them personally that he was sorry, and were even exploring the possibility of forgiving him. Nobody could have expected them to go that far, but they did.

Whether these actions will actually lead to forgiveness by all is anybody's guess. The media circus that ringed the scandal may have accelerated and distorted the process in some key respects. There were clearly some imponderables. How contrite really was Imus? Only hours before his visit with the team, Imus had been told that his popular, high grossing show, the source of his pride and national identity, was history. Did news of that strike the team as sufficient punishment and make them more open to forgiving him? If not, were there other penalties they would require? Were some prepared to grant him pardon simply on the basis of his apology while others need him to do much more in order to make up for what he did to them? What is the calculus of justice in such complex circumstances? Does a one-shot meeting between a celebrity offender and players who are young enough to be his granddaughters do more to promote or to prevent the greater good?

Forgiveness usually relies on repaying the victim in one form or other, yet the justice expected in response to quite similar infractions can differ widely according to cultural settings and special circumstances. Determining what Person X would need from the offender, Person Y, in order for pardon even to be considered, might entail, as in the return of the stolen ring, gestures of contrition, such as a willingness to remove some burden from the victim; civil and religious codes that dictate set penalties; and social and cultural conventions, such as the Puritan practice of placing miscreants in the stocks. All of these attempts to mete out justice contain a large measure of arbitrary figuring that arises from the peculiar assumptions that various traditions make about the price of crime. There is an argument, too, between those who believe that only proper justice can usher in forgiveness and those who think justice too often acts against forgiveness.

Jonah, that fishy prophet from the Hebrew Bible, adds still another twist. What if God jumps in to forgive those whom you're trying your best, on God's orders no less, to read the riot act in the name of justice? That is exactly what happened in the ancient tale. As you'll recall, Jonah was dispatched by God to the big, unruly city of Nineveh to warn the people to forsake their wicked ways, the exact nature of which are left to our imaginations. Jonah found the assignment distasteful and disobeyed instructions, booking passage on a trading ship bound for Tarshish. God fixed Jonah's wagon by causing him to be tossed overboard, where the famous fish gobbled him up. Confined to smelly surroundings in the fish's tummy, Jonah got religion, as it were, and pleaded for forgiveness and a quick exit. God obliged by having him spit up on shore where, chastened, he set out for Nineveh to do his job.

The hapless Ninevites took it on the moral chin from Jonah. He followed the script, delivering a withering critique of their ways. Don't be surprised, he said, if the whole urban area is crunched because of this bad behavior. For some reason, they paid attention and grasped the point that this was indeed a major

emergency. Staring with none other than the king, they put on sackcloth, the well-known symbol of repentance, and begged God for mercy. And they got it. God forgave them.

One thing that lends authenticity to biblical stories is that they don't end the way we would ordinarily expect them to. Here, for

---

Apparently he saw himself as the messenger of doom and gloom, predicting that divine justice would soon unleash a calamity on them. Never did it occur to him that God would step in with forgiveness.

---

example, Jonah had preached the word of judgment, much as he initially didn't want to, and the ending seemed to turn out superbly. The city repented and God forgave. But as we see, Jonah responded by being hopping mad. It wasn't his idea of a happy ending. Apparently he saw himself as the messenger of doom and gloom, predicting that divine justice would soon unleash a calamity on them. Never did it occur to him that God would step in with forgiveness before this disaster could unfold as payment for Nineveh's sins. Did he think God had made a fool of him?

forms of anti-Semitism. The concept may be judged inadequate on many grounds, but one of its precepts remains exceedingly valuable: punishment must fit the crime.

Can anyone doubt that whatever else "God's will" might signify, it surely includes a survival instinct that yearns to make things right? An "eye for an eye" gyroscope seems to spin within us, seeking balance no matter what steps we might take after that. It is important here to note that the formula wasn't taken literally. "Eye" and "tooth" ("tooth for a tooth") were symbols for both Babylonians and Hebrews. The payment could take many forms, including money. Sometimes that objective can be essentially achieved, as when a painting that has been stolen from my living room has been returned in perfect shape and the crook has been prosecuted through the courts. In

other situations, the return payment would be much harder to figure. If the thief who stole my painting also viciously assaulted my grandmother during the break-in, placing compensatory value on that damage would be theoretical at best.

Everett Worthington, the forgiveness scholar at Virginia Commonwealth University, defines the purpose of justice as restoring power to the victim. "The crime reduces the power and status of the victim," he wrote in an essay for the Fordham University *Urban Law Journal*. "A victim's sense of power can be reestablished through balancing the social books (for example, by restitution or incarceration of the offender) and balancing the emotional books (for example, by seeing esteem-lowering acts by the offender or through publicly humiliating the offender). In each, raising the

Professor Worthington engages his class in the science of forgiveness.

esteem of the victim increases the victim's relative power either by seeking revenge or seeing the criminal punished." By comparison, forgiveness is for Worthington a gift of love, freely given.

Justice may be accomplished without forgiveness, but forgiveness is hard to imagine without some degree of justice that bolsters the victim. The elements blend variously from person to person who has suffered the indignity. One example of that mixing is the Rev. David Tinney, a United Methodist pastor. In 1992, according to an account in the *Seattle Times*, Tinney was training on his bicycle for the annual trek from Seattle to Portland, Oregon, heading downhill at 30 miles per hour when a car driven by an 18-year-old girl edged up beside him. A teenage boy reached out of the passenger side and shoved Tinney. He hurdled over the handlebars and onto the street, suffering long-term injuries, including a punctured lung, a fractured right arm, and five broken ribs.

Tinney proclaimed his forgiveness of the two young people in his next Sunday sermon and invited congregants to join him to discuss the subject over a ten-week period. His behavior might have been taken as a function of his job as a minister. Clergy are often pigeonholed as the "professional Christians" who perform feats of saintliness that other Christians either don't believe themselves capable of achieving or are too busy to be bothered about. Not only is that a mistaken portrait of members of the clergy, who indeed tend to suffer every misstep that human flesh is heir to, but also to Tinney's particular conflicts. He was able to forgive the teens, though they never owned up to their crime. But before and after the trial that convicted them, he remained disturbed that such a wanton act had inflicted lasting disabilities on him—that he was, in Worthington's terms, weakened and in need of justice to reestablish himself.

"There can be good use for anger," he told the paper. "Anger can point us to seeking justice. It's when anger turns to bitterness that it crosses the line." He said reading and prayer were primary tools in helping him to "stop wanting to retaliate, stop blaming," and start forgiving. "You can still be angry with the act, still seek justice for the crime, but separate the person so the person isn't associated with the deed." The bouts of anger had continued through the forgiveness stage, he said. The justice he desired was tempered by that forgiveness. His intervention with the court spared the two teens from serving time in adult prison.

At their first meeting in the office of Tony's attorney, Ples Felix recalled in his interview for the film that "We looked in each other's eyes; we shook hands; and [Khamisa] let me know, after I expressed my condolences and sympathies and my need to support him and his family, that he didn't hold any animosity towards me or my family, that he had forgiven Tony, and that he had determined to start a foundation that will stop kids from killing kids. And he asked me point blank, 'Will you help me?' and I said, 'Of course. That's an answer to my prayer.'"

How much that moment owed to the fact that justice had been done is difficult to tell. That it had something important to do with it seems beyond dispute.

"RESTORATIVE JUSTICE" SHOWS PROMISE AS A NEW WAY

A prime meeting ground for forgiveness and the law is called "restorative justice." Worthington's article, quoted earlier, was part of a major conference on the subject that became the basis for the June 2000 edition of the Fordham *Urban Law Journal*. The title of the symposium, "The Role of Forgiveness in the Law," placed the challenge front and center at a time when many Americans were rethinking the state of the conventional legal system.

That concern doesn't necessarily become a welcome mat for forgiveness among lawyers and judges, however. There is an abundance of suspicion that a pardoning sentiment can hamper the rightful goal of hard-nosed justice. It is often deemed too soft and too permissive to be let into the courthouse. In recent years, the tough-on-crime mentality appears to have grown even stronger, with maximum sentences and three-strikes-and-you're-out rules having become more common. In the midst of a wave of vengeance, the fans of restorative justice have had their work cut out for them.

To its advocates, restorative justice opens the judicial process to methods that can heal the alienation and fractures arising from crime and may change the outcome of criminal proceedings. It is not enough to settle the material scores, they say; we must mend the human brokenness that broadens the destruction. Such methods, they add, have an honorable history within earlier societies, including widely separated communities of indigenous people.

"We can compare restorative justice to the traditional system as follows," said David M. Lerman, a former assistant district attorney and head of a task force on restorative justice in Milwaukee, during the Fordham conference. "The traditional system asks three questions: Who is the perpetrator; what law was violated; and how do we punish that person? Restorative justice asks a different set of questions: first and foremost, what is the harm that has been caused; secondly, how do we fix that harm; and third, who is responsible for that repair?"

Not much restoration can happen in the proponents' view without genuine repentance. The trick is to tell what's "genuine" from what isn't. The word is, watch out for the imposters who possess great acting skills but lack sincerity. Be alert to those who apologize only to gain favor from the court. Jeffrie Murphy spoke of this sleight-of-tongue by quoting Montaigne on the subject of the fakers: "These men make us believe that they feel great regret and remorse within, but of atonement and correction or interruption they show no sign. I know of no quality so easy to counterfeit as piety." Murphy is among those, however, who maintain that repentance isn't absolutely needed for forgiveness to go forward. Likewise, say he and other practitioners of restoration, beware of confessions or apologies that may be extracted by force or threat.

Generally speaking, restorative justice involves getting offenders together with victims on neutral ground. Lerman has condensed the agenda to three steps: talking about exactly what took place during the offense; allowing everyone to explain how the incident has affected them; and discussing what would be needed to fix the damage.

The traditional system asks three questions: Who is the perpetrator; what law was violated; and how do we punish that person? Restorative justice asks a different set of questions: first and foremost, what is the harm that has been caused; secondly, how do we fix that harm; and third, who is responsible for that repair?

"These conferences allow a victim or community member to ask questions that they need answered in order to begin to clear up the 'distorting effect' the crime has had on their lives," Lerman said. "Thus, this process sets up the possibility for the victim to gather information and personally assess the offender in order to forgive him/her. Nevertheless, forgiveness does not mean letting an offender off the hook. Punishment in the form of incarceration may still occur; being accountable in other ways that more actively repair the harm are also established. Sitting across from someone you have victimized is often more difficult than facing a judge for 15 minutes during sentencing."

Lerman's concept of restorative justice rests on a set of principles. They include placing the needs of victims first; recognition that breaking the law fractures human relationships; an offender's willingness to own up to the crime and show personal growth through the restorative justice process; and an earnest effort to fix the damage.

As Lerman then illustrated, the principles lead to vastly different outcomes. One case featured a woman in the Midwest who had been beaten nearly to death by a pair of men when she interfered with their attempt to steal her car. Both men were sent away for long prison terms. Three years into their sentences, the woman began visiting one of the men and was eventually moved to forgive him because, in part, she said she had grasped the fear that gripped him. But he should remain in prison, she said, for the sake of community welfare.

The other case involved an 18-year-old girl who had stolen $1,000 from her employer, a department store. Lerman explained that the girl's mother was a cocaine addict who often disappeared from home for days at a time, leaving the younger brothers and sisters on their own. In addition, her brother was in prison. After she was caught, she met with two officials of the store who listened to her ardent apology and the painful circumstances of her home life. Affected by her testimony though somewhat distrustful, they asked her to speak to a series of sessions for newly hired employees. She did. Lerman provides the coda: "Her case was ultimately dismissed."

Proponents of a human-relations approach to justice contend rather persuasively that it keeps those caught in initial offenses from committing far more serious crimes. The following story may be evidence of that kind of deterrence, though it's only possible to speculate. In 2005, a Waukesha, Wisconsin, man was arrested for a hate crime. Police said that the man had been drinking at a bar and was driving his pickup truck when he and his passenger spotted an African American man with fishing gear crossing the road ahead. Furious at having to stop his truck, the man pulled out a handgun and waved it in the man's direction. The passenger then released his German shepherd, ordering the dog to chase the man.

The gun-toting defendant was in line for a stiff prison term before his African American victim agreed to a restorative justice session with his tormentor. The men reportedly shook hands, and each found dignity in the other. The offender went through sensitivity training and alcohol treatment. At the trial, the victim pleaded for leniency for his offender, asking that he not be given jail time because, in the victim's words, "He's not the same person, and that means a lot to me." The judge gave the offender a relatively mild sentence: two years probation including 30 days in jail and 200 hours of community service, half within agencies that focus on African Americans.

"The system of justice cannot bring forgiveness into people's lives," Worthington told the restorative justice conference. It was for him more than a sensible affirmation. He had personal experience. The tragedy of his mother's savage murder had shaken him to the core. It exposed him to a terrifying dose of reality that severely tested his own ability to envision the act of forgiveness as a benefit in keeping with the assumptions underlying his research. Adding to the anguish was the ruling by the court that freed the alleged murderer from prosecution on a legal technicality. He had found it possible within himself to forgive his mother's assailant, he told the conference,

> There is a place for forgiveness in the justice system, but it is background, not foreground.

and in that wrenching process he'd discovered that the justice system can play a vital role. It could "provide opportunities that make forgiveness and reconciliation more or less likely. Forgiveness needs to occur person by person by person—in the hearts of attorneys and judges, in the hearts of victims and perpetrators, in the hearts of community members. There is a place for forgiveness in the justice system, but it is background, not foreground." It may produce conversion experiences or, more commonly, plea bargains that lessen the severity of the punishment.

THE FINE LINE: REJECT VENGEANCE, BUT KEEP MERCY HONEST

A yellow caution flag seems worth waving at this point.

The desired alchemy between forgiveness and justice depends on an authentic exchange between an offender's repentance and a victim's acceptance of it. It's all about quality and timing. If the crime has dealt you an insult and/or taken a chunk out of your dignity, Murphy emphasized at the conference, then you must refuse to block the resentment that comes from being a victim and must resist forgiving too easily or quickly. Hasty pardon can signal approval of the crime, the very opposite of what might be intended.

"There has in recent times been much cheap and shallow chatter about forgiveness and repentance," he said, "some of it coming from high political officials and some coming from the kind of psychobabble often found in self-help and recovery books. As a result of this, many people are, I fear, starting to become cynical about both." Forgiveness becomes less likely in a climate where "too many claims of repentance are insincere and expedient."

Within the scope of religion, Judaism's practices of forgiveness contain the most sophisticated code of justice. When a wrong is done, a precise series of steps is prescribed to make restitution. Having followed the initial rule by admitting the infraction, the wrongdoer is instructed to confess and express remorse in public and vow never to do it again. The victim must be paid back in whatever way is deemed appropriate. And a plea for forgiveness must be voiced three times, if necessary. The intention of this thorough procedure is clearly as much communal as it is a resolution

of injustice between two parties. It understands that the crime has ripped the fabric of community life and that a restoration of that brokenness is as important, if not more important, than repairing the offense itself. Without attention to the relationships that make up communal solidarity, hatreds breed hatreds rapidly and in isolation.

An example of how that tradition could be adapted to modern circumstances was highlighted at the conference by Frederick W. Gay, a lawyer from Des Moines, Iowa. Two youthful self-styled neo-Nazis had terrorized a local synagogue, causing much physical damage to the building and stirring great fear and outrage among members. Holocaust survivors in the area reportedly went into hiding. Against this backdrop, Gay, an advocate of restorative justice, contacted the rabbi to ask if he would consider talking with the two offenders. He recalled the rabbi's first response: "Why would we do something like that? I'm so mad I could strangle those two." Gay says he asked the rabbi to think it over, and two days later the rabbi called him back to say: "That's what we ought to be doing. It is not what my heart says, but I think that is what we ought to be doing."

According to Gay, the first tentative step was a meeting in the basement of the synagogue between the two perpetrators and seven members of the congregation. They heard each other out—the young men described their backgrounds and the congregants explained the impact the synagogue attack had had on Jews. They struck a deal. The young men agreed to do six months of service for the synagogue and to attend classes in Jewish and Holocaust history taught by the rabbi. As the talks proceeded, friendship blossomed among them.

Along the way, the young men asked for forgiveness. The response from the synagogue groups was that they needed to fulfill the requirements for atonement in the manner prescribed by Judaism. The offenders followed that guidance and spoke with great feeling about how sorry they were for having caused such harm. The rabbi and the other members of the group felt a powerful note of sincerity coming from the young men. They saw a turnaround in the offenders' attitudes and spirit that would keep them from repeating such crimes. Confident that the young men had met the conditions of atonement, the synagogue's members granted them forgiveness and celebrated the surprising bond that had developed among them. The wrong suffered by the synagogue had been acknowledged, restitution was offered by the offenders, and the criteria for forgiveness

were satisfied. It was reasonable to assume, therefore, that the change witnessed in the young men and in themselves would benefit everyone and the whole community.

With these rewards potentially available, why would anyone refuse to welcome the customs and rituals of forgiveness into the judicial process?

I think of that question often while driving past the county jail close to where I live. For many years the century-old jail was bursting at its seams from a steady influx of mostly drug users. The county began farming prisoners out to more rural prisons at a per diem rate. The strategy for fixing the overcrowding was, predictably, to build a huge addition to the existing jail. The county's first plan involved demolishing homes on a residential block. After heated protests from the neighbors, the plan was revised, the houses spared, and the expansion went forward by going upward. Costs continued to spiral, reaching a total of nearly $30 million. That was two years ago. The new facility is already overcrowded.

Why, then, in the face of enormous human and financial costs, wouldn't something like restorative justice become a more appealing strategy for dealing especially with lesser crimes? There are many reasons, of course, not the least of which is that the booming prison industry and lucrative anti-drug operations have an obvious vested interest in keeping things as they are. But in addition to those government-funded enterprises, there are two factors more closely related to the individual.

One is risk. Seeking resolution beyond the strict application of the law involves face-to-face encounters with those who have inflicted pain and suffering upon the victim. The victim's desire to protect himself or herself against further trauma may make a meeting with the offender unthinkable. If it is to be the honest exchange that is deemed necessary, the victim may fear having the resentment and anger that has served as the first line of defense either taken away or trivialized. Letting go of raw feelings can be experienced as a loss of face. Having felt insulted and denigrated by the crime itself, the prospect of being cut down ever further can be frightening.

The alternative is to live with those slights and sores. Nothing in the studies done by the scholars suggests that there is anything to be gained in holding on to the hatred and anger longer than may be necessary to express legitimate outrage. And the studies say there might be much to lose. Those such as the synagogue members, who have taken the risk of exposing their negative feelings and hearing the testimony of the accused in the basement of the temples, are usually thankful for what emerged by taking that path—blessing for the individuals involved and for the greater community. The initial willingness to let down one's guard can reap great benefits. But particular circumstances guide whether anyone is capable of taking those steps.

The other factor is skepticism over whether choosing the restorative process will water down the application of justice. Will the offender's infractions be treated more lightly than if there were no background efforts to achieve forgiveness? Will the victim be cheated out of proper restitution by being asked to see the offender as a human being of equal worth?

Often the victim can be so degraded that stark legal penalties and material settlements

---

Why, then, in the face of enormous human and financial costs, wouldn't something like restorative justice become a more appealing strategy for dealing especially with lesser crimes?

I introduce them sometimes to others or even just tell them stories of people I know and what they've done. I'll never set myself up there to be a healer to people who have endured a pain that I have never endured.

WORKING WITH OFFENDERS

What we have to move away from is just inflicting pure punishment and pain on offenders. We have come into a very punitive mindset about prisons; and just the tip of that iceberg, of course, is the death penalty. But if you attend hearings in legislatures where they're considering legislation, all the mentality is to punish people—to take the pound of flesh, pain for pain, make them suffer for what they did. That's the punitive aspect. We have lost the sense that what prisons ought to be is places for restoration of human life.

I don't know that the word *forgiveness* will ever be used by the criminal justice system, but we might begin to see prisons as places for restoration of human life. Every year the equivalent of the population of Seattle is released from prisons in the United States. We have 2.1 million people in prison. Educational programs are being cut, and the Pell grants were cut. "Why should they be going to college? The victims didn't get to go to college!" Congress cuts the Pell grants, so people aren't educated.

What happens to human beings in an environment for 10, 15, 20, 25 years, where they're not developed as human beings and then they're released? Have they become more human or less human? And will that reverberate back on us in more violence? I'm almost certain it will, unless we as a society understand that word *for* and *give*. Instead of automatically thinking we have to make you experience pain because you caused pain, we have to look at the whole of us, and what's good for the whole of us, a sense of wholeness, of healthiness, and of restoring life.

Seven

The Two-Way Street

The simplest case of forgiveness is when a clear line separates victim from violator. Someone has done the harm and someone else has been harmed. Matters are often more complicated, however. Everyone suffers at the hands of others and causes those others to suffer: there is enough blame to go around. Forgiveness may require at least two to tango.

When the Beatles broke up in 1967, fans around the world collapsed into despondency and grief. Most probably were aware that rock bands on average had a relatively brief shelf-life and that even the sensational lads from Liverpool wouldn't stay together forever. Unlike the bickering and sullenness that accompanied some endings, however, the Beatles' split seemed rather calm, notably free of finger-pointing and public squabbles over who was to blame. Many observers felt the surface peace was largely due to the death of their manager, Brian Epstein, who was credited with having kept them together and catapulting them to universal acclaim.

That explanation was another way of saying that Epstein had been able to keep the lid on a boiling cauldron of personal frictions that might otherwise have driven them apart much earlier. We can only imagine what might have caused the Beatles to give up the most sensational gig in music history. It does them no disservice or dishonor to say that they were as human as any other foursome in history who had banded together for any purpose. This musical spectacle consisted of batch of young, energetic, talented men from a laboring-class neighborhood in Britain. Over a dazzling, furious, and unimaginable career, their gaze was so uniformly fixed on the trajectory of the rocket that was lifting them to greater heights of success that they naturally overlooked the potentially destructive tensions and differences among themselves. Even with Epstein's masterful handling, those sharp edges couldn't be entirely rounded off and eventually took a toll, as they do in most any foursome. There were no doubt a host of factors in the decision to end the band, from weariness to separate ambitions to artistic disagreements, but nothing must have mattered more than the tangle of gripes, both petty and prodigious, that had grown up like thorns to create greater and greater distances from one another. It certainly wouldn't have been unique to them, but from what we know now it applied to them.

Furthermore, we may assume that John, Paul, George, and Ringo all contributed to this web of conflicts and personal tensions. The catalog of hurts and slights and jealousies had room for all of their listings. Everybody must be supposed to have had a part in creating the problems. That would have presented a host of opportunities for everybody to exchange apologies and forgiveness with everyone else.

We speak here of a two-way street of forgiveness.

That is where we have a lot in common, hypothetically, with the Beatles. We have experiences that leave us guilty for doing something to someone else and at the same time convinced that the other person was guilty too. This is the realm of the everyday experience with friends, family, and coworkers, as well as strangers. I have a car accident and am angry at another driver for running into me. I'm sure it's the other person's fault, and the police report points that way. There can be no doubt the other driver was going too fast to stop in time. If the begging for forgiveness doesn't come from the other person, I'll at least collect recompense from his or her insurance company. In the back of my mind, however, I'm naggingly aware that I actually hadn't come to a complete halt at the stop sign and that, even though nobody saw the infraction, it probably contributed to the crash.

Truth is, we're both guilty of causing this thing to happen. An apology from the driver might help justify the version of the story I prefer, but in reality we both are responsible. If justice and forgiveness were truly sought, they would need to be pursued mutually, each party seeking the equivalent of honesty, an expression of regret, restitution (in whatever form), and pardon from the other. That's a difficult and unlikely outcome, but circumstances that challenge us to achieve such two-way resolutions constantly place us in such dilemmas.

Up to this point in the book, the primary focus has been upon the one-way street variety of forgiveness. One person has done something wrong against another—or persons against many others. The violation is clear: for example, you have stolen my chickens. It is, in that sense, the good guys versus the bad guys.

We have experiences that leave us guilty for doing something to someone else and at the same time convinced that the other person was guilty too.

The good guys have been hurt, and the bad guys owe them something like an apology and/or the returned chickens, and the judge has determined the legal penalties. Forgiveness may follow if the violated person feels able to do it, depending on lots of things, such as the sincere repentance of the violator. In any case, the responsibilities and functions are quite clear. Often, these are the high-profile cases—the murders and kidnappings and betrayals that jump out from the media and tend to define our concepts of justice and forgiveness.

The Limits of the "Good Guy, Bad Guy" Storyline

One-way street episodes, magnified by a barrage of television news reports and endless specials, reinforce the state of mind known widely as the "victim mentality." Much has been written about this tendency to see ourselves as the unwitting, innocent, and hapless victims of a vast range of things, from the government to junk food. There are, of course, good reasons for this sense of being at the mercy of others' designs.

Powerlessness stems from two major influences. One is that political and economic power has become more concentrated. "Bigness" and impersonal bureaucracies have gained more control over our lives. The other reflects a central theme in Robert Putnam's book, *Bowling Alone*, that heightened individualism among Americans has increasingly caused us to shy away from various kinds of community life in favor of isolated activity, bowling by themselves rather than on teams. Given those forces, it is understandable that people feel weak and powerless. Blaming others or blaming faceless institutions is a natural response. Mass society simply engenders a readiness to see Big Brother or Large Sister as responsible for the ills that beset us. Branches of psychotherapy that encourage self-absorption and personal fulfillment often contribute to this phenomenon by convincing patients that the negative, poisonous feelings that hold them back are inflicted by faulty parents or other suspects. Within the self-fulfillment movement, the goal of liberation from the forces of repression and suppression is a matter of recognizing the harm done by others without our consent or participation. We become free by ridding ourselves of the obstacles others have placed in our way.

Obviously there is a great deal of truth to this. The reality of victimhood has too often been denied and ignored. Others planted poisonous thoughts in our minds and abused us long before it was considered acceptable to discuss problems with friends and counselors. The denigration of women created generations of battered psyches even as the women themselves denied or explained it away. The change in climate toward more openness has made it possible for many women to acknowledge that, in fact, they were victims; and this has allowed them to escape the trap. Likewise, sexual abuse of children has come out of the closet, revealing a small army of people who were once too frightened to talk about it. So there are whole categories of real victims who belong to that one-way street category. There is nothing contrived about it.

Yet the trend has led to excesses. Examples of the one-way street dynamic expose us to real victims, but they also generate a copycat effect. It's perhaps easiest to see with regard to celebrity or sensational crimes. Laci Peterson is murdered. Her husband is convicted. Television coverage goes wild. In the background is the shadow of O. J. Simpson, who escaped criminal guilt but, in the public's mind, largely remained his former wife's killer. The obsession with these cases hugely magnified their significance, but beyond that they reinforced the increasingly common fear of becoming the target of attack. The clear-cut offender-victim scenario, while applicable to those situations, plainly doesn't fit the description of most of the messes we get into from day to day. But victimhood has an allure precisely because we identify with those actual victims and perhaps

feel tempted to fit ourselves into a similar scenario because it creates such sympathy and attention. Though the chances of undergoing a similar fate may be extremely remote, the dramatic crime may call up memories that invite the comparison. Someone watching a guest on Oprah detail a gruesome story of abuse by her husband may allow the viewer to recall something that is, in fact, similar, or to adopt a victim's framework for interpreting something quite dissimilar. Further complicating matters, a lonely person's cry for attention is different from someone who claims victim status as a means of shirking personal responsibility or the self-hating soul who strives to play the role of a celebrity-victim. In any event, victimhood is catching.

Actual victims deserve every scrap of our empathy and support. The problem arises when that model carries over into our lives to the extent that we overlook or misread situations in which we are both victims and offenders in weaving a pattern of bad behavior. If the victim mentality takes hold, it becomes difficult if not impossible to see one's own responsibility for what Sir Walter Scott called the "tangled web." Separating true victimhood from the kind that is borrowed from

---

The problem arises when that model carries over into our lives to the extent that we overlook or misread situations in which we are both victims and offenders in weaving a pattern of bad behavior.

---

one-way publicity to excuse personal wrongdoing is a tough assignment. Even so, neglecting that task can be even more costly.

The two-way street is like a pyramid scheme that has collapsed. Everyone who has been financially wrecked by the swindles could correctly blame the person who suckered him or her into it. Then again, the victim has probably suckered other people into the get-rich tornado; that makes the victim a conspirator. And so on. In the end, everybody was at some time both guilty and innocent. If all these participants were willingly gathered together for the purpose of making amends, the result, ideally speaking, would be a somber exchange of apologies and some beginnings of forgiveness. Ideally speaking, that is. The point is that everybody would have a history of having been misused by someone else and having subsequently misused others. The fact that the scheme's guidelines demanded this sort of behavior would be lamentable but not an excuse for claiming only victim status.

A glaring sign of victimization gone-too-far is when people take it on by association, although there isn't a clear and present threat. Disease has often been that triggering device. Dire outbreaks are forecast based on scientific probabilities, inciting widespread public fear among many who imagine themselves vulnerable to the invisible scourge. Bird flu, for example, was projected as a worldwide pandemic in the year 2006. It never happened that way, through no fault of the professionals who rightfully sounded the alarm; but the prospect of this epidemic fostered that variety of victimization known as hypochondria.

AMERICA, VICTIMHOOD, AND FORGIVENESS

America has its own particular susceptibility toward victimhood. Deeply ingrained in our history is the conviction that America was founded by the will of the Almighty to be a "light to the nations," a special messenger of democracy and freedom. This special mission, blessed by God, at best has been a challenge to live up to noble principles and at worst a claim to superiority over the rest of the world. When natural or human disasters strike America, therefore, questions arise over who could have caused such things to happen to God's favored people. Among the explanations, ludicrous to many, is that God inflicts these punishments because people have flouted divine morality. Another, however, is that a satanic power of indefinite identity has attacked America in order to destroy its divinely constituted character. President Bush's comments after 9/11 that the terrorists struck because they hate our "freedom" sounded like that refrain, as did his reference to the "axis of evil" that is out to destroy our special status. Thus, we become victims because of our greatness, though the ultimate source of this vengeance remains uncertain. The horrors of Hurricane Katrina in 2005 serve as another example. Within the flood of coverage given this terrible event was a certain amount of innocent astonishment that such disasters could happen to America, as if God's protective shield should prevent them. A year before, the gigantic tsunami in Southeast Asia killed hundreds of thousands more people and destroyed vast amounts of property. But while Americans were shocked and saddened, some didn't see it as violating the natural order or as an assault on a people who had been blessed with a special divine favor. As terrible as the tsunami was, it wasn't the same as a calamity visited upon us as a special nation. On one level, this view expresses a reverence for America that is deserved and inspiring. On another, the image of ourselves as "special" goes overboard and allows us to see ourselves as victims of diabolical designs rather than as players who have ourselves contributed to the problem.

The Doblmeier film highlights this "mystery offender" phenomenon in its segment on the 9/11 horrors. The principals in the film have lost loved ones in the attack, and we feel deeply for them. At first it seems clear that these victims blame the terrorists for their loss, as one might expect them to. The terrorists are more of an unseen force rather than a mental picture book of actual murderers. Then the anger becomes focused on the decision by the city to remove the piles of rubble containing fragments of human remains to Fresh Kills on Staten Island. The source of the distress becomes rather amorphously the city, but the victims do not specify who did what and why it was wrong. As the colossal tragedy played itself out, the claims to victimhood apparently became more generalized. The film's other reference to unspecified oppressors is the Garden of Forgiveness in Beirut. It invites visitors to sort out the maze of perpetrators and victims for themselves without implicating anyone directly.

Sometimes the one-way street becomes two-way. When I was in high school, the little church we attended was rocked by scandal. The treasurer of the church, a quiet, pleasant woman, had been stealing from the offering plates. This was a church whose members were mostly factory workers, so the Sunday collections were meager to start with. In this

The Garden of Forgiveness in Beirut, Lebanon invites visitors to sort out the maze of perpetrators and victims for themselves without implicating anyone directly.

nickel-and-dime congregation, every bit counted. The treasurer, it turned out, had robbed the church of at least $35,000 over the course of a few years, though it was impossible to tell for sure because much of the collection was in cash. Shock and anger quickly engulfed the congregants. Some demanded her arrest and conviction. Mercy was at a premium. Then came a revelation. Her husband was a chronic gambler who had run up staggering debts. Her pilfering of church funds was a desperate attempt to keep shady creditors from seeking savage revenge.

In the minds of most church people, the revised story didn't excuse her from what she had done. That was wrong. But she wasn't the only one to blame. She had stolen in an effort to forestall a grisly outcome that would have destroyed the couple's good standing. Though she might now be considered an "enabler," her husband had wreaked havoc. With this multifaceted picture in hand, the church revised its course of justice. The church did not press charges against her but chose to work out a payback plan. The husband, unable to rely on her subsidy, was soon in jail.

The public dramas—the Peterson murder, the Columbine shootings, the Amish school massacre—have a dual effect. We might assume

> Anyone who has provided counsel to people over an extended period of time could fill volumes with examples of how anger and resentments sprout up between and among people in the course of everyday interactions.

that, on one hand, they awaken some in the audience to dark corners of their own lives where their own victimhood hides, and that the big-screen event prompts them to bring it to the light of day. Otherwise, the one-way street hype, by emphasizing victimization, can lessen chances that other viewers will be willing to look at their own complicity in the crises that have emerged in everyday life.

I suppose anyone who has provided counsel to people over an extended period of time could fill volumes with examples of how anger and resentments sprout up between and among people in the course of everyday interactions. It may be impossible to trace the deep-seated animosities to a single source, but the spark can be a relatively insignificant incident. A slight is detected and never resolved. A parent insists that a child play soccer. A business partner lands a lucrative client by skirting the company rules. These incidents, in turn, may have been prompted by previous slings and arrows from the other person. Before you know it, there's big trouble, and no one person is at fault.

Close relationships of family and friends spawn most of these sinister tangles, as we all know. For the sake of survival, many of the ongoing annoyances among spouses, parents and children, rock groups, and prayer groups are best ignored or overlooked. The dinner table habits of parents irritate kids to no end, but using such wincing moments as building blocks of major resentment seems a bad idea. These habits rank among those behavioral tics that are almost never directed at anyone but come with the basic biological and psychic equipment of the parent. In other words, it's not exactly intentional. Same goes for the occasions where Mom or Dad shows the new significant other the pictures of little Suzie or Billy naked in the bathtub. An expression of embarrassment and friendly disapproval is well in order, but otherwise I think we do well to move on.

Real resentments usually involve something important, like money. Three years ago, Dear Abby responded to a tempest in a jug that had the earmarks of the little thing that became a big thing. The plaintiff, signing in as "The Unforgiven in N.H.," explained that she and her husband of a year placed their loose change in separate water jugs. She began snitching some from his, she confessed, with every intention of paying it back, naturally. But she hadn't gotten around to it, when once day her husband claimed she'd lifted $250 from his jug. She said she felt awful about what she'd done and was paying off her debt since then, but he kept swearing at her and calling her a thief. Now she was down in the dumps and wondered if life between them would ever be the same.

Abby probably didn't need to remind "Unforgiven" that "the honeymoon is over," but she did so, perhaps as a precaution. Then, in good two-way street fashion, she took "Unforgiven" to task for dipping her hands in hubby's jar and implicated him, too. "What you did was

wrong," she wrote, "but *so is cursing one's spouse and nursing a grudge.*" Abby added, "One of the secrets to a happy marriage is learning to forgive each other. If yours is going to work, the two of you must accept that neither of you is perfect and learn to negotiate beyond your disagreements."

HUSBANDS AND WIVES

Marriage is no doubt unrivaled as a setting for combat. It is a garden overrun with weeds. On that subject, former President Jimmy Carter was forthcoming about the two-way street character of his marriage during a recent interview with "Speaking of Faith" radio host Krista Tippett. Jimmy and his wife, Rosalynn, were approaching 61 years of marriage (adding, "if we stay together the next four or five months"). He agreed with Ms. Tippett that spats among people who know each other are much more intense than those we might have with strangers.

"And you're involved with them permanently and inseparably in a way," Mr. Carter said. "So you have to learn to accommodate idiosyncrasies—or from a personal point of view the faults and mistakes of another person—and do it without ceasing. As you know, when Peter came to Jesus and kind of bragged about how he was forgiving, he bragged or said, 'Should I forgive seven times?' And Christ said, 'Forgive seventy times seven times,' which means without ceasing."

For his own marriage to work, Mr. Carter said, he and Rosalynn had to avoid trying to "dominate" one another by giving the other plenty of space. It had been mighty difficult to do, he said. He also recited the old adage against going to bed angry at each other. As a preventative and proscriptive measure, Mr. Carter said that the two of them had read the very same chapter and page of the Bible aloud together every night for the past 30 years. "So, you know, I would say that giving each other plenty of space and becoming reconciled as best we can—I don't say we are perfect at the end of every day—no matter if we did have some differences during that day, then that is what has helped us to perpetuate our marriage, plus love for each other."

A couple I've known for a long time, immigrants from the Ukraine, turned their marriage into advanced pugilism from day one. They circle each other looking for an advantage, deal setup jabs, then wade in for the haymaker whenever the opportunity arises. They aren't in the habit of apologizing for low blows or anything else they might have used to attack. Yet I doubt they've ever seriously thought about splitting up. Their partnership is, in the words of a mutual friend, "the most indestructible bad marriage I've ever seen."

There is a hall of fame unto itself, consisting of all those who stick together in spite of or because of their history of grievances and counter-grievances for which they have rarely if ever sought resolution, let alone forgiveness. Among the luminaries in this dubious museum are the principals of two well-known movies. The *Lion in Winter* features the irascible twelfth-century monarch, Henry II (Peter O'Toole), locked in eternal combat with Eleanor of Aquitaine (Katharine Hepburn), his wife and chief tormentor. *Who's Afraid of Virginia Woolf?* consists of a drunken night in the life of George (Richard Burton) and Martha (Elizabeth Taylor), whose toxic exchanges deliver wound after wound without destroying each other—quite.

Each tale of marital bleakness is built upon layers of accusations, defensive retorts, and reprisals whose basic content remains the same, though the years have changed the form in which they are expressed. Separated as they are by centuries and the details of their personal warfare, the two couples share a common bond. When blame from both sides never relents or submits itself to justice, mutual confession, and forgiveness, the flickering of love that can still be still seen faintly between them will never grow into a joint flame to light their way. They are stuck.

As usual in such combat, the origins are difficult to pinpoint. In *The Lion in Winter*, it might have been Henry's suspicion that Eleanor had slept with his father. Few things set off a chain reaction more than that sort of incident. The

---

When blame from both sides never relents or submits itself to justice, mutual confession, and forgiveness, the flickering of love that can still be still seen faintly between them will never grow into a joint flame to light their way. They are stuck.

---

actual record isn't made clear. It is certain that Eleanor tried to stir up a revolt against Henry, not a terribly wifely thing to do, but we aren't sure what Henry might have done to provoke it. Nonetheless, Henry tosses her into the castle prison, where she has languished for ten years at the time of the story. For his part, Henry is a rogue and a bully whose explosive temper has

wreaked havoc on all around him, including the couple's three sons, who are clamoring for the right to become the next king. Henry, his mistress in tow, is in a muddle over whom to choose to succeed him. He prefers the youngest son, John, but Eleanor is pulling strings for the eldest, Richard the Lionhearted. It is against that backdrop of political and personal tension that the titanic battle between Henry and Eleanor takes place and old scabs are picked. Both are brilliant schemers with resumes crammed with betrayals and plots, towering personalities determined to fight until the bitter end. They spar with the greatest of the never-give-an-inch champions. Eleanor's famous quip understates it beautifully: "Well, what family doesn't have its ups and downs?"

In *Who's Afraid of Virginia Woolf?*, George and Martha have burrowed into their existence at a small college, where he teaches history and she endures as the undutiful wife. Her father is president of the college. He took a shine to George when the couple was first married, eyeing him as a bright, shining candidate to become the next president of the institution. But both father and daughter had soured on George and ridiculed him as a failure. George, for his part, had done little to dispel those judgments. The resentments that had grown from this acid soil were unavoidable, perhaps, but at any rate they obviously weren't avoided. George had succumbed to the lure of a winning proposition and paid a heavy price for it. That wasn't the worst of it. The couple rips at each other incessantly during the night, infected by the madness of blame. The madness has no clear beginning and no promise of ending by any resort to the mending ministry of repentance or forgiveness. It is a shield against abysmal rage and the frantic attempt to assign personal misery and their misery together to the other person. To provide some buffer against this reality, they have "invented" a son. This fiction provides an outlet for the remnants of devotion, channeling hostility that might have finally destroyed them into a mutual, if mythical safe house. It is the precarious island that has preserved them.

Martha's description of its function is thus: "The one thing, the one person I tried to protect, to raise above the mire of this vile, crushing marriage, the one light in all the hopeless darkness—our son."

The heart of the movie is the unmasking of this fantasy to reveal the yawning chasm of reality. George creates a story of a car crash to "kill" the son.

Through the fusillade of dark, fiery eruptions, however, hints of love make brief, fragile appearances, like blades of grass popping through concrete. The screaming tantrums and bouts of treachery cannot completely stamp love out. Glimmers of affection suddenly peak through the armor. "You know there's only been one man in my whole life who's ever made me happy?" Martha confesses. "Do you know that? . . . George, my husband, who is good to me— whom I revile, who can keep learning the same games we play as quickly as I can change them."

Likewise, Henry and Eleanor attack each other with the ferocity that seeks not so much to destroy as to tame. Each regards the other as grotesquely magnificent. Nobody will come

---

Through the fusillade of dark, fiery eruptions, however, hints of love make brief, fragile appearances, like blades of grass popping through concrete. The screaming tantrums and bouts of treachery cannot completely stamp love out.

---

near replacing either in their lives, though they are destined never to reach a threshold of forgiveness that will allow them to go beyond paralyzing animosity.

Indestructible bad marriages. But are they beyond redemption?

While the odds appear heavily against redemption, the obstacles are never insurmountable. Escaping the vicious cycle of the two-way street certainly requires an extraordinary shift within the psyche and soul.

John Adams and Thomas Jefferson, the second and third U.S. presidents, illustrate the potential for undergoing such a reversal between them. As historical drama, no story of public figures exceeds it. During the earliest years of the republic, while both were principal actors in the country's formation, they became bitter political rivals; Adams the staunch proponent of a strong federal system, Jefferson the spokesman for a decentralized America of small shopkeepers and farmers. The conflict also reflected the wide culture gulf between Adams's Puritan Massachusetts and Jefferson's aristocratic Virginia, which had shaped their distinct styles, both Adams's frugality and Jefferson's ostentation.

The feud continued unabated for many years after both had left office and retreated to their homelands to grow old. Then one day Adams heard news that one of Jefferson's children had died. Adams wrote to his old rival to express his sorrow, noting that loss of his own children added to his sympathy for Jefferson. The heartfelt nature of that overture and Jefferson's readiness to accept Adams's compassion broke the long impasse. The old warriors joined in a spirited correspondence in friendship. The saga doesn't end there. In one of the most poignant of coincidences, Jefferson and Adams died on the same day, July 4, 1826.

For a breakthrough to happen, for the years of compounded blame to break down, a change of will and direction must take place. That experience often goes by the name of "conversion," whereby the inner components of one's being undergo a mysterious realignment so that nothing ever looks the same again. It can be an overwhelming "Damascus Road" experience like the one that transformed Saul the persecutor of Christians into Paul the Apostle of Christ, or a quiet recognition that a crack has appeared in the wall of hatred and self-defense. Something fundamental happens to remove the fierce determination to see the other as the cause of our misery and to make us consider our role in the thickened hostilities. Many of those who go through such a shift in mind and heart cannot account for it; others insist that we can be open and ready for it but cannot make it happen; still others believe it is the fruit of prayer and meditation. Not everyone wants it, of course, which only adds to the mystery. Is it always better to desire to untangle the knots between and among quarreling parties ("intimate enemies," as they are called elsewhere), or is it possible to die in peace without absolving and being absolved? The answer for most people lies within the religious heritage they claim. And every single major religious tradition comes up with the same response: nothing beats forgiveness and restoration as a path toward spiritual fulfillment and moral responsibility. That is not always considered welcome news, however.

Where there's a will, there's a way, says Thomas Moore. While it's possible to prepare the way, Moore said in his film interview, forgiveness cannot be commanded or plucked like a rabbit from a hat. "We can't control the dynamic of what forgiveness is," he said. "So that means that forgiveness itself by its definition, its essence, is not something that someone does. Forgiveness is a condition, or is a state, or it's even a gift. It's a kind of grace, you might say. It's almost a theological thing, a spiritual thing that comes of its own when we have done what is required to allow it to appear."

So, though we don't know when we might be swept up to heaven, we can at least keep our bags packed and our shoes shined.

> Every single major religious tradition comes up with the same response: nothing beats forgiveness and restoration as a path toward spiritual fulfillment and moral responsibility. That is not always considered welcome news, however.

WHEN THE WISE AND THE GOOD FORGET THEY DO WRONG

Readiness is especially difficult for those who regard themselves as too smart or too morally superior to admit their wrongs. The competitive jousting within most work settings only stiffens that refusal to give ground. It's there, amid the striving for recognition, reward, and prestige, that the two-way street resentments become entrenched and often denied. It is widely presumed that people with above-average intelligence and church-going ways are above committing petty offenses, to say nothing of big ones. The other half of the assumption is that they don't hold grudges, because "high minded" folks don't hold grudges. Add to that the notion that admission of guilt or the practice of forgiveness will appear as weakness, which can lessen your chances of winning the prize. Nothing fails like the appearance of weakness.

A psychology department in a southern liberal arts college comes to mind. It was comprised of six professors who pursued a wide variety of specialties. Four had been together for more than a decade, and two had arrived within the past five years. Though they weren't the Mouseketeers, they got along well and some close friendships existed. The point of friction was how to rotate the position of chair of the department. The regular term was three years, but for reasons of death and circumstance, the pace had become disrupted. Actually, nobody wanted the job because it imposed heavy administrative duties that none of them had a hankering for. One professor in particular had gone to some lengths to avoid it. She had been lecturing extensively at other institutions and building an impressive reputation in her field of developmental psychology—and she had no intention of giving up these outside activities. Her colleagues decided it was her turn, however, and she agreed. But she determined to do it her way, by spending almost no time in the office and operating mostly from home. It sure looked like the passive end of aggression, whereby she was exacting vengeance without saying so. Nobody else did so,

either, but the anger against her neglect built. By the time her term was up, the animosities had metastasized for lack of being treated in the first place. Though the department still looked civilized from the outside, its inner life was in shambles. When it came to selecting the next chair, the logical candidate was a veteran professor who had long felt he had never received his rightful respect at the college. Though he had shunned being chair because he felt it was a thankless task that would only add to that disrespect, the woeful performance of the incumbent chair gave him an idea. Why not, he reasoned, use what power there was in that job to boost his career? Nothing else had worked, after all. The other element was that he blamed his colleagues for installing the weak, ineffective current chair.

A year into his term, the climate in the department had, if anything, worsened. Whereas his predecessor was literally remote, she had continued to canvass her colleagues for their opinions on major policy matters. The new chair's version of remoteness was quite different. He showed up with every intention of demonstrating to the faculty just how a department was supposed to be run. Their advice to previous chairs had only mired the department in a quagmire, he believed, so it was up to him to run it by himself. Besides that, he thought they held him in low regard. He virtually halted all department meetings and made unilateral decisions, breaking his friendly ties with other professors. Quiet shock settled in. The rest of the faculty suddenly felt as if they were his enemy. In an effort to build power and reputation, he initiated projects that brought him credit by bypassing his colleagues. Their passive-aggression stirred further resentment in him, and he began to reduce their pay increase increments in return.

Matters never came to a head. By the end of his term, he had almost no contact with the other professors. By the same token, the others had willingly assented to this course of events without a major whimper. Years later, those among that group of professors who remain are hard pressed to recreate the history of that dark era. Only attrition by retirement and moves to other institutions brought some new life to the department. At the time of crisis, none could confront the monster at the door. According to the script, the educational elite is not supposed to stoop to gutter fighting. So very often they don't—and pay the consequences. Two-way street justice and forgiveness never becomes an option.

The same goes for the inner sanctums of religion. When overt political ambitions are driven underground by the demands of "propriety," they inevitably produce venom and rage. Leaders of religious groups have unfortunately been willing to be looked upon as the exemplars of their faith without the warts and doubts of religious pedestrians. This arrangement of having a "professional religious" class means that the laity need not be so concerned with the letter of the law. They have leeway when the professionals agree to do it for them. The danger, of course, is that clergy become hoisted on their own petards. Their interactions sometimes create feuds of colossal proportions. The grand

---

Leaders of religious groups have unfortunately been willing to be looked upon as the exemplars of their faith without the warts and doubts of religious pedestrians.

---

old man of evangelical Christianity, Billy Graham, once told me that in his estimation there was no politics quite like church politics in its intensity and subtlety. For good reason. When you can't duel openly, you do so through all sorts of subterfuge. Ill will is a natural outcome of this kind of tussle for authority and renown, and evidence has shown that many clergy have had the capacity for fierce disputes that go untreated.

The turmoil in the Episcopal Church over homosexuality and women in the priesthood has churned up much two-way street hostility that has only grown in scope and vindictiveness. The church's decision to ordain gay candidates set off the trouble. The consecration of a gay bishop added hugely to the tensions, and the election of a woman presiding bishop has sprinkled more fuel on the fire. The church has begun to fracture in the United States, as spokespersons on both sides hurl invective at each other. The live-and-let-live pluralist tradition within Anglicanism—the world movement of which the Episcopal Church is a part—is being stretched to its limits.

Breaking the Cycle, Mindfully

If the time for appeasement and reconciliation does arrive, the sublime wisdom of the revered Buddhist, Thich Nhat Hanh, becomes particularly relevant. Getting off on the correct foot means practicing the right thinking moment by moment. "Right thinking goes in the direction of understanding and compassion, and wrong thinking goes along with discrimination, hate, violence," he said in his interview for the film. "And your thinking is your most concrete expression of yourself. Your thinking, your speaking and your action. And every thought that you produce bears your signature."

Imbued with the "mindfulness" that Buddhism espouses, everyone can discern what

---

"Right thinking goes in the direction of understanding and compassion, and wrong thinking goes along with discrimination, hate, violence. Your thinking is your most concrete expression of yourself. Your thinking, your speaking and your action. And every thought that you produce bears your signature."

---

is good. "You are producing beautiful right thought or not," he said. "You are producing beautiful right speech or not. You are producing right beautiful action or not. If you are mindful you know that your thoughts, your speech, your action are right or wrong. And if they are right they have the power to heal, to nourish you and the world. And that is enough as a guide to your daily life."

The wreckage of the past need not ruin us, he added. "There might be wounds that have been caused in the past that are now still unhealed. And if you know how to live deeply in the present moment, you can touch the wound of the past and heal it. Because by action of the present moment you can prepare a good future, and you can also repair the wrong that has been done in the past."

Eight

Repairing Divided Houses

How different would America be if a massive effort to mend the outrages of slavery had been set in motion soon after the Civil War? As it was, the shakily surviving Union undertook a project of social and economic repair that was essentially a thin stopgap initiative, lending some material and welfare support to freed slaves and to the devastated South. But what if, in addition to that, the United States had attempted something similar to South Africa's "truth and reconciliation" process, which, more than a century later, brought accusers and victims together after the collapse of that nation's brutal apartheid regime? Black and white South African leaders agreed that the forging of a new biracial nation depended on clearing away the decades of mounting hatreds, so they took the risk and sought public, face-to-face accounting of the crimes against humanity.

HOW MUCH TRUTH
CAN WE TAKE?

America in the nineteenth century was a world where the idea of an extensive human rights and justice campaign in the aftermath of a monstrous war, even one based largely on ending slavery, simply didn't exist. With its emphasis on public assistance and the granting of political freedom, in theory at least, Reconstruction was about the best that could be expected (most Iraqis would probably settle for the fulfillment of such promises from the United States now). We could scarcely imagine former slaveholders confessing their atrocities to their ex-slaves or seeking mercy from those they had once bought and sold like sacks of grain. Still, it seems worth wondering whether a coordinated attempt to defuse racial and sectional hatreds might have slowed or contained the cancerous spread of racism.

Such speculation assumes that the South African experience has yielded substantial benefits; and I do make that assumption, based on a welter of testimony including a rich store of anecdotal material. Accounts of bestial treatment of blacks at the hands of apartheid's white enforcers mingle confessions of guilt by the torturers with the stricken looks of victims reliving the depths of their pain. Out of this has come amnesty for those judged to have told the truth and a lifting of fear and vengeance from those who suffered so egregiously. How much good was done, however, is anybody's guess. Success and failure are largely in the eyes of the respective beholders. It is widely assumed that the "Truth and Reconciliation" project, the seventeenth of its kind tried in recent years, helped South Africa become a biracial society less torn apart by the past, but the extent to which it helped and how it did so remains unclear. Perhaps hope itself that the process would achieve favorable ends predisposed many to view the results in a positive light.

From the first, some skeptics saw little or nothing of value coming from the process. One of them, the well-known apartheid foe, writer, and artist Breyten Breytenbach, scoffed at the process during a recent lecture in Senegal, describing it as a band-aid approach that only disguised greater evils. Calling it a "sinister farce," Breytenbach dismissed the assumption that "'confessing' to torture and repression is intended to lead to an absolution supposed to bring about 'reconciliation.'" He continued, "This must be a prime example of practicing the hypocrisy of religious motivations as snake oil for social leprosy in order not to lose the essential: the power and privileges of the rich and those whom they co-opt."

It will doubtless take decades to grasp the impact of this bold move, but in the brief time since the dramatic hearings took place, popular opinion appears to support the process as a means of promoting the nation's health. If that consensus holds on the basis of further historical evidence, then Americans have good reason to speculate that this country might have averted some of the worst atrocities of Jim Crow, even at a time when reconciliation wasn't an option in the collective unconscious of that age. Then came the final obliteration of Indian resistance and the physical and psychic carnage that it left behind untended, to haunt us still.

Where is forgiveness in these national and global conflicts? All nations and peoples get fractured sooner or later, or so it seems, either from internal or external forces. Rebellions, ethnic revolts, greed, repression, and religious zealotry are among the causes. Societies rupture or continue to exist with slaves and masters or mythically contrived superiors and inferiors. Independence rent India, dividing Hindus from Muslims. The Moors broke the relative uniformity of Spain, creating lasting enmity, after which Spain crushed the integrity of indigenous people in present-day Peru and

Mexico in its lust for gold. General Chiang Kai-Shek's mainland Chinese army, defeated by Mao Zedong, overran the Formosan people, subjugating them. The rulers of Sudan wage genocide against their own people in Darfur. A history of untreated tensions in Rwanda led to the slaughter of an estimated 800,000 Tutsis by Hutus in 1994. After the shell of a "united" Yugoslavia was shattered, the old lines of religious sectarianism reemerged, pitting

---

All nations and peoples get fractured sooner or later, or so it seems, either from internal or external forces.

Orthodox Serbs, Catholic Croatians, and Bosnian Muslims against one another. On every continent, fractures have appeared and reappeared as the underlying hostilities remained, with few exceptions, untreated.

Societies that are unwilling or unable to address the sources of hostility reflect on a large scale what transpires on an interpersonal level when animosities become frozen in a cycle of vengeance. On either level, where there is no "give," there is no cure; no concern for truth, no clarity. "We need to remember, I think, that a nation is simply a collection of individuals," Marianne Williamson told the film's interviewer. "That's all that it is. So whatever psychological and emotional truths apply to an individual, apply to a nation. If you never have the courage to be brutally honest about yourself, you're not going to grow. That's true of an individual and it's true of a nation." Americans divide into two camps, she believes: those who think the United States does nothing right and those who believe the nation does nothing wrong. "These are both not just wrong," she said, "they're wrong-minded." She urges, instead, a "fearless moral inventory," as suggested by Alcoholics Anonymous.

Sorting out common "truth" that is agreed upon by one or more sides as a step toward reconciliation is at best a spotty and elusive accomplishment, always incomplete and open to dispute. Fortunately, however, a shared history of chronic quarrels isn't necessary to move toward an easing of the hatred. The other role belongs to reality. That is, if a nation or people does nothing to alleviate the forces of destruction and to lower the fevers of vengeance, then the survival of the whole country or region may be at risk. A grasp of that reality can overcome deficiencies in getting the history right or fixing blame. A sword of Damocles hangs over the collective head and will likely fall if nothing is done to reduce what the renowned preacher Harry Emerson Fosdick referred to as "warring madness" (in his hymn, "God of Grace and God of Glory").

Northern Ireland: Tentative Hope in a "Benign Apartheid"

Northern Ireland is submitted as Exhibit A on the reality chart. The centuries of bad blood between Protestants and Catholics in that region have left deep physical and mental gashes on both sides. While most of the origins of the conflict lie with the British oppression of the Irish, the deadly conflict in recent decades has also had a life of its own, the two sides exchanging blows in vengeful succession. All the while, some remarkable individuals and groups of courageous people worked to plant seeds of harmony between the two sides by creating safe zones where they could begin hearing one another's accounts. The best known of these individuals were the winners of the 1976 Nobel Prize for Peace, Betty Williams and Mairead Corrigan, founders of the Community of Peace People (originally the Northern Ireland Peace Movement). Theirs and similar small projects kept vigil through years of continued killing and halting attempts to forge a political solution.

God of Grace and God of Glory
Harry Emerson Fosdick

God of grace and God of glory,
On Thy people pour Thy power.
Crown Thine ancient church's story,
Bring her bud to glorious flower.
Grant us wisdom, grant us courage,
For the facing of this hour,
For the facing of this hour.

Lo! the hosts of evil 'round us,
Scorn Thy Christ, assail His ways.
From the fears that long have bound us,
Free our hearts to faith and praise.
Grant us wisdom, grant us courage,
For the living of these days,
For the living of these days.

Cure Thy children's warring madness,
Bend our pride to Thy control.
Shame our wanton selfish gladness,
Rich in things and poor in soul.

Grant us wisdom, grant us courage,
Lest we miss Thy kingdom's goal,
Lest we miss Thy kingdom's goal.

Set our feet on lofty places,
Gird our lives that they may be,
Armored with all Christ-like graces,
In the fight to set men free.
Grant us wisdom, grant us courage,
That we fail not man nor Thee,
That we fail not man nor Thee.

Save us from weak resignation,
To the evils we deplore.
Let the search for Thy salvation,
Be our glory evermore.
Grant us wisdom, grant us courage,
Serving Thee Whom we adore,
Serving Thee Whom we adore.

When on Good Friday, 1998, a settlement was announced, those cottage industry peace groups deserved much credit for keeping hope alive. The Good Friday Agreement was also evidence that the light bulb of reality had been switched on by two intractable foes that foresaw nothing ahead but the further demise of their homeland if killing didn't cease. In the previous three decades, 3,600 Protestants and Catholics had been murdered. Like the other guys or not, there was a better alternative.

The Agreement meant that the cycle of violence could be broken. Despite a setback in 2002, during which the Agreement was suspended, the negotiators pressed on. On May 24, 2006, in a scene that boggled the eyes of old partisans, Gerry Adams, the president of Sinn Fein, the Catholic political arm of the Irish Republican Army, and Ian Paisley, the hitherto recalcitrant leader of the Protestant Unionist Party—enemies as bitter as ever walked the earth—sat together at a joint news conference to announce a plan for the two sides to share power. Adams wouldn't shake Paisley's hand but promptly proposed the 80-year-old Presbyterian minister as the shared government's first minister. Paisley refused but was only playing hard to get. Less than a year later, in his new capacity as overseer of

the power-sharing process, Paisley appeared jointly with the prime minister of the Republic of Ireland, Bertie Ahearn. Fittingly, or appallingly, Paisley presented Ahearn with a musket from the Battle of the Boyne in 1690, in which the king of England, William III, a Protestant, had defeated the deposed English king, James II, a Catholic. In his remarks, the old, grizzled warrior said, "We must not allow our justified loathing of the horrors and tragedies of the past [we won't forget!] become a barrier to creating a better and more stable future for our children [hint of forgiveness?]."

Northern Ireland was clearly on a new track, but what did that mean among the row houses of Belfast and along the country byways? Even before the latest breakthroughs on the political front, Robert Enright and his colleagues at the International Forgiveness Institute in Wisconsin believed the road ahead to a genuinely tolerant, shared Northern Irish society was long and painstaking. Not long after the Good Friday Agreement, Enright and his wife, Jeannette, created lessons about forgiveness for children in the schools of Northern Ireland. They have sought to incorporate their project into the larger peace movement.

At the grassroots level, the strains between Catholics and Protestants were dire. Bill Shaw, a Presbyterian minister in Northern Ireland who is a leader in efforts to find unity, said that the hope and trust that had crested after the announcement of the Good Friday Agreement had mostly vanished. "Protestants and Catholics still to a very large extent live totally segregated lives," he says in the Doblmeier film. "They go to different schools, they shop in different shops. They socialize in different bars. We are talking about a benign apartheid."

The Enright approach focused on forgiveness within the classroom and in the playground. Dr. Seuss's books have helped open up the subject, along with aids such as "forgiveness glasses," which, when put on, suggest a kinder, gentler way of seeing someone in need of forgiveness. Artwork is employed. Stories are read. The day-to-day sticky wickets that children encounter are explored. Enright has been impressed with the ability of teachers and children to speak to these issues with an astounding depth of resourcefulness and good will.

"Forgiveness glasses," such as those worn by this Northern Irish girl, were used as a means of adopting a new view that could overcome Catholic-Protestant bias.

Professor Enright pauses next to a "Lest We Forget" sign.

remain largely hidden both physically and mentally from the American mainstream? Is it, as in Sigmund Freud's conception, a repression of that which the nation has declined to look at in all its brutal reality? If circumstances had been more favorable to a forgiveness approach, perhaps someone like Enright might have made a difference. Maybe a curriculum could have been designed for the emerging network of public schools that would have brought about a more amenable atmosphere. It is obviously a matter of speculation. But so long as there were people of good will who had the same forgiveness resources of the Bible and the wisdom of the ages, an approach like that need not have been inconceivable (I don't mean here that Indians were obliged to convert to Christianity as the price of admission—that demand by many victors remained a severe obstacle). The fact is that it didn't happen, and the result was that the resentments and dehumanizing attitudes found expression in an assortment of destructive behaviors that continue to this day. It stands out in bold relief as a reminder of what happens when the opportunity to create mending is ignored or goes unrecognized.

As the result of having changed the legal status of both African Americans and Native Americans without changing their human status

in the eyes of the dominant culture, both groups were locked into a demeaned, dehumanized, second-class citizenship. For African Americans, inferiority was encoded in Jim Crow laws. The U.S. Supreme Court's school desegregation decision in 1954, *Brown v. Board of Education*, again altered their legal status while the racism behind their treatment by the dominant society went largely untouched except by Dr. Martin Luther King Jr. and other civil rights leaders. The job of excavating and untangling the generations of estrangement and resentment posed a mammoth challenge that might have been considerably reduced in scope by a nineteenth-century version of truth and reconciliation. For Native Americans, the symbol of everything that gave rise to the deep hostilities was the reservation. Reservations were, in effect, more detention camps than enclosed enterprise zones, shrunken refugee lands often deemed worthless. This was the lot of proud people, many of whom, in all fairness, had accumulated ill will toward other tribes in endless cycles of warfare, much of which was unresolved. But the bigger tragedy was that, collectively, they were a defeated, diminished people who were reduced to producing trinkets and, like Chief Sitting Bull in Buffalo Bill's Wild West Show, to playing the stereotypical "noble savage."

Slavery came close to breaking the Union, but the nation survived as a political entity. However, it became even more divided over the rights and treatment of blacks. The blood had barely drained from the Civil War battlefields before a rigid racial caste system was under construction. Statutory racism became slavery in a different guise, enforced by social mores and white supremacist legalities. Race had become the "American dilemma," the phrase used by Swedish sociologist Gunnar Myrdal in the title of his groundbreaking 1946 book on the subject. The damage incurred from centuries of injustice in a nation that had never seriously endeavored to make amends was incalculable, a powder keg set to explode claims to national integrity and corrode the body politic.

quieter forms of destruction eat away at the nation's substructure. The United States allowed the crusade to consign African Americans and Native Americans to sanctioned inferior status to charge ahead virtually unimpeded for nearly a century following the Civil War. The 1954 Supreme Court school desegregation decision became the flashpoint for the stirring civil-rights campaign to free African Americans from segregationist oppression. Dr. King channeled the pent-up anger of an abused people into a nonviolent movement to end that abuse, echoing the Bible's appeal to forgiveness and reconciliation. For most of those who had suffered under white domination, the most immediate goal was justice, a removal of the laws and the symbols that had demeaned

---

"He who is devoid of the power to forgive, is devoid of the power to love."—Martin Luther King Jr.

A country that isn't roused to combat human rights abuses within its own borders is naturally less willing to confront the ongoing inequalities and sources of grievance. Without an immediate threat to peace and security, the opportunities for achieving understanding and compassion become far less urgent. Thus, the

their humanity. Forgiveness was understandably not the first order of business, although Dr. King had sown the seeds of a nonretaliatory consciousness that kept that possibility alive. Meanwhile, the store of unresolved racial distrust continues to keep America from realizing a fuller potential, and to that extent discontent jeopardizes national survival.

power and money; on the other, exclusion and poverty. Yet they went ahead.

From the start, the South Africans essentially debated two questions: what was needed to make life in the nation something other than a reverse of white domination, and if redemption and reconciliation were to be tried, what was their source? Was it primarily the principle of justice—eye for an eye prosecution, on the order of the post-Nazi Nuremberg trials? Or would it be the fulfillment of democracy that would trust black majority rule with righting wrongs and knitting together a new national unity? Or was it the oldest wild card in the book, the power of forgiveness based on something like faith? *Forgiveness* proved too strong a term. The scars of savage repression hadn't healed enough to embrace that option. At the entryway to forgiveness, however, were the more immediately sensible steps of the two sides facing the truth of what had happened and thereby making possible reconciliation.

"Realists" had always scoffed at the forgiveness path as a fuzzy-minded, softhearted solution to tough problems. The improbable, impractical faith alternative had never gone away, however; and to the world's astonishment, South Africa pulled out the old map and began using it to steer a course away from vengeance.

Nelson Mandela, the political messiah of the new South Africa, proclaimed the rudiments of this revolutionary plan not long after the white apartheid regime had folded. He recalled the original incentive behind truth and reconciliation in a July 3, 1999, article in the *Guardian* of London. "Reconciliation is central to the vision that moved millions of men and women to risk all, including their lives in the struggle against apartheid and white domination," he wrote. "It is inseparable from the achievement of a non-racial, democratic and united nation that affords common citizenship, rights and obligations to each and every person, while it respects the rich diversity of our people."

The degradation and poverty forced upon millions of blacks by the imperious white government must not only be remedied but also be kept in memory, Mandela said, adding: "We recall our terrible past so that we can deal with it, forgiving where forgiveness is necessary—

The degradation and poverty forced upon millions of blacks by the imperious white government must not only be remedied but also be kept in memory, Mandela said.

---

but not forgetting. By remembering, we can ensure that never again will such inhumanity tear us apart, and we can eradicate a dangerous legacy that still lurks as a threat to our democracy." Looking back, he saw flaws in the process, but he insisted that "about this there can be no equivocation: recognizing apartheid's evil lies at the heart of the new constitution of democracy."

The other grand figure in the truth and reconciliation process, Archbishop Tutu, took a more radically Christian stand from the outset, declaring that nothing short of forgiveness would suffice. Speaking on Bill Moyers's program, *NOW*, in 1999, Tutu advocated a position that said, "'I am abandoning my right to revenge, to payback. By the fact that you have abused me, you have hurt me, you are—whatever it is you have done, you have wronged me. By that you have given me a certain right over you that I could refuse to forgive you. I could say that I have the right to retribution.' When I forgive, I say, 'I jettison that right, and I open the door of opportunity to you to make a new beginning.' That is what I do when I forgive you."

Could genocide and torture be forgiven? Moyers wondered.

Tutu: "As a Christian, you have to say, 'Are there things that are unforgivable?' I'm afraid

> "'I could refuse to forgive you. I could say that I have the right to retribution.' When I forgive, I say, 'I jettison that right, and I open the door of opportunity to you to make a new beginning.' That is what I do when I forgive you."

we follow a lord and master who at the point when they are crucifying him in the most painful way can say, 'Pray for their forgiveness.' And we follow the one who says 'Forgive one another as God and Christ forgave you.' That is for us the paradigm. We may not always reach to that ideal, but that is the standard."

He included himself. The archbishop said he'd often been "angry, very angry" about the sufferings of apartheid's victims and had directed much of that rage toward God. But South Africa had demonstrated that no situation was without hope and forgiveness.

The Truth and Reconciliation Commission functioned between 1995 and 2001 as an alternative to courts of justice. The focus was on the victims. They were brought into open hearings to tell of the cruelties inflicted by the enforcers of the barbarous system. The agents of this brutality were then invited to apply for amnesty by promising to tell the whole truth amnesty was "hell for most victims' families" but also convinced that it was "the precondition for peaceful transition of power." The greatest benefit of the commission, he wrote, was to expose the perfidious lies "that do such harm that they can poison a society just as there are a few lies in private life that can destroy a life." The truth and reconciliation process had "rendered some lies about the past impossible to repeat," Ignatieff asserted, and thereby defined a standard that could be used to judge the behavior of the new black majority as well.

Grace, beyond Reason

As the hearings wound down, a prominent member of the commission reflected on its mixed results. Pumla Gobodo-Madikizela, a psychologist who had focused on human rights violations, noted that the process had left many South Africans soured and discouraged. Some victims felt that their testimony had been in vain. The small supply of money set aside to compensate some of them had been "too little, too late," she said. Offenders were living in shame, having had their crimes exposed.

Yet she saw something else going on in the lives of those who felt "an incredible sense of validation," she wrote in the *Boston Globe* in 1998. "For these victims, nothing was more affirming than an opportunity to break the silence about the brutality they suffered during the years of apartheid."

The hearings had made possible a direct face-off between victims and offenders that never would have taken place in the official courts of law. And something even more. "Herein lies one of the commission's successes: the requests for forgiveness made by some perpetrators and the granting of forgiveness by some victims and survivors. This is unprecedented in this history of atrocities in the twentieth century.

"The commission's final and greatest success," she concluded, "is that violence was averted and South Africa did not plunge into a spiral of revenge following the end of apartheid. For that, everybody can be grateful."

Reconciliation was already showing signs of concrete progress. The deadly antagonisms between former black freedom fighters and the old white power structure had begun to give

---

"For these victims, nothing was more affirming than an opportunity to break the silence about the brutality they suffered during the years of apartheid."

way to common efforts. As one observer put it, they didn't necessarily love one another, but they were willing to cooperate for the good of the nation.

Nothing on a national stage could overshadow the luminous stories of personal courage and grace that emerged from the process. In her book, *A Human Being Died That Night: A South African Story of Forgiveness*, Gobodo-Madikizela relates one of the most powerful of those experiences, which borders on being an epiphany.

Gobodo-Madikizela tells of one of apartheid's most notorious butchers, Eugene de Kock, appearing at a hearing to seek amnesty for some of the killings for which he was responsible (he'd already received 212 years in prison and two life sentences for crimes not covered by amnesty). De Kock had been in charge of assassinations and death squads. At one point in the proceedings, he asked to meet in private with some of the widows of men he'd put to death. To the astonishment of the onlookers, the women agreed. During the highly charged session, de Kock apologized and asked the widows to forgive him. They did. Unconditionally, they told Gobodo-Madikizela, because they believed his apology was heartfelt. As he had spoken, they were crying. "I want him to know," one of the women told the author, "that, although we were crying, our tears were not only tears for our husbands, but they were tears for him as well. I want to hold him by the hand and to show him that it is possible to change."

Later, Gobodo-Madikizela met with de Kock to ask why he had apologized. At once he began to shake, and she describes him as a broken man. With tears in his eyes, she writes that he said, "I wish I could bring them back. I wish I could say, 'Here are your husbands.' But unfortunately I cannot do that." Without thinking, she reached out and touched his hand.

Journey toward Forgiveness

Martin Doblmeier went on the road as a filmmaker and returned as a confessor.

It happened during his tour of the country with his new film, *The Power of Forgiveness.* The routine was simple and nerve-wracking for the producer: show the film to diverse audiences to sample their reactions. It was the inevitable moment of truth.

So Doblmeier, founder of Journey Films, scurried about the country screening his new documentary like a proud papa holding up pictures of his newborn, hoping the folks out there would like it. In his sweep, he showed the film in three dozen venues, including the United Nations, to 15,000 viewers.

They liked what they saw. Doblmeier could set aside any lingering doubts he might have had, however absurd, that something might have crept into his work that would drive people screaming through the exits. No, the response was hugely positive, for which he was thankful.

UNFINISHED BUSINESS

But something else caught his attention even more. At stop after stop, people lined up to tell him that the documentary had roused thoughts and memories of their own struggles with forgiveness. They wanted to unburden themselves of the pain and anguish that had been stirred. Feelings of regret, resolve, anguish, anger, and grief poured out on the man who had, unwittingly for the most part, caused it to happen. Doblmeier had become an agent for purposes he had not foreseen. To this impromptu flock he had become a confidante, a consoler, a counselor, and a liberator. Some told him the film had given them hope that old grudges that had pressed down on them like inner anvils could be overcome. Others spoke of betrayals that they had sealed away within themselves. Lots of unfinished business had resurfaced. Still others eagerly explained their struggles to

forgive. The ordinary movie preview, in other words, had become an exercise in extraordinary self-disclosure. Doblmeier stayed as long as it took after the movie was over to hear them out.

"I became more gentle and understanding," he said. "I'm here to open a film and I find that it opens wounds for people. I didn't go out to set an agenda; I just came to realize that people were hurt."

He immediately thinks of the elderly man at Elizabethtown College who waited until everyone else had left before approaching him. A couple had just left after telling Doblmeier how a young man had molested their teenage daughter in a restroom. The perpetrator had also done the same with another girl, and the prosecutor was calling for harsh penalties. But the parents felt compassion for the young man and argued instead for him to receive counseling. After searching far and wide, they found a lawyer who would represent their merciful convictions and eventually won their plea.

As the parents left, the old man stepped forward. "What about me?" he cried out. "What do I do?"

With anger rising in his voice, the man blurted out that he had lost his brother in the Korean War. Every day since, the man had

Martin Doblmeier, director of The Power of Forgiveness.

hung the American flag in front of his house to honor his brother. Doblmeier heard a man still consumed with some kind of guilt over his brother's death.

"Why was he so mad?" Doblmeier wondered. "Was it because he let his brother go to war? Or the way he died? Or that he was missing?" He suggested to the man that maybe he'd done enough for his brother and that it was time to move on. His words left no apparent impression.

"He walked away and started crying," Doblmeier recalled. "He's carrying something that he can't let go of."

Faced with so much testimony unrelated to the film per se, Doblmeier didn't shrink from the challenge or pose as a spiritual or psychological healer. He stood there and listened, feeling, he said, "like a pastor": not a pastor, he hastened to add, but "like" a pastor.

"When people come up after a showing of the film, I can't help feel responsible," he said. "They are open about their hurt. I don't think of myself at the center of it. There is something in the film that spoke to them. If they feel some trust in me, I feel honored to hear them. I want to help people to be heard. I'd spend as much time as possible with them, but the issues they are bringing up could never be resolved in a few minutes.

"I try to let them find their own answers; many I feel have needed to be confirmed in their own instincts."

Martin Doblmeier's inner and outer qualities create a strong, unobtrusive presence. A six-footer with a shock of blondish hair, he walks with a purposeful, forward-leaning motion that bespeaks his eagerness to tackle the next riddle. On the day we met, he was wearing black slacks and a black short sleeved shirt, a combination that ordinarily projects seriousness; for him a seriousness about ideas and aesthetics rather than himself. He searches the subject matter of his films like a prospector sifting dross for nuggets of gold, carefully and thoughtfully. He approaches his sources with curiosity and a low-key amiability that puts them at ease, but also with an eye for pretense and hypocrisy. That is, he is understated in the sense that someone with the requisite intellect and human skills can afford to be but usually isn't. By necessity, he's also an accomplished multitasker. As honcho of his own production company, he is called upon to do everything from raising the funds to promoting the goods. But what drives him is a need to understand how religion makes itself known in the world.

He has been on the move for more than three decades, compiling an intriguing assortment of 25 films, including the widely praised *Bonhoeffer*, a portrait of the German theologian Dietrich Bonhoeffer, who was killed for plotting against Hitler. He did another profile of the late Cardinal Joseph Bernardin of Chicago, who won widespread affection for, among other things, his enlightened leadership, his forgiveness for a man who falsely charged him with sexual abuse, and his courage in the throes of an agonizing death.

Doblmeier studies his subjects with a fixed, attentive gaze, small inquisitive eyes, and a calm demeanor that signals that he's paying attention. He's devoted his professional life to catching lightning in a bottle, that is, to capturing the invisible realities of the spirit world in sights, sounds, and images that will evoke them, or something close to them, on the screen. The subject is "immaterial and infinite," he noted, but then again, so are the possibilities when it works. His fascination with religion took flight during his years at Providence College. He majored in it and made it

the subject matter for his films. In theological terms, he looks for signs of the spirit in earthly forms. In Christian tradition, Jesus Christ is understood as the "spirit made flesh" or "God made man," the one-time revelation encapsulated in the doctrine of the Incarnation. Doblmeier, then, might properly be described as an incarnationist who searches for latter-day manifestations of that larger revelation.

His two associates, Dan Juday and Adele Schmidt, closely collaborated on the project over the five years needed to complete it. Together, they swapped ideas for ways to capture the elusive subject that stemmed from his own stories of learning and experience. Juday did many of the interviews; Schmidt's sharp eye for telling footage matched film clips with appropriate sound bites.

Filming forgiveness proved difficult for Doblmeier and his crew. Like other religious subjects he'd tackled, he called it a "hard medium to work with." Fiction allows a creation of scenes that simulate forgiveness, and many films have depended on such moments to supply the dramatic power. Not so with real life, where such experiences are rarely enacted with cameras rolling. Usually, the reporters arrive after the two sides have reconciled, and the brief slice of time in which transformation has taken place has gone. The onlookers must be satisfied with explanations after the fact.

Science, Spirituality, Security

As Doblmeier sorted through options for discussing forgiveness in fresh ways, his operating assumption was that the possibilities could be both spiritual and scientific. At the August meeting of minds on forgiveness in Atlanta in 2003, the forgiveness scholars from social science had made a strong impression with their measured studies that demonstrated the health benefits of giving up anger and resentment. The self-help forces stood next to the "Jesus said so" religious advocates in a display of solidarity never seen before. The secular and the religious formed a united front of sorts, though there were many areas of previous overlap. Many of the empirically minded scholars were personally rooted in faith, and others in the religious camp were pleased that doing God's will lowered their heart rates a few notches.

Doblmeier attended the Atlanta powwow, struck by the potential that this loose partnership held. Maybe it would make a good film. When he started work on the film in 2005, he was on the lookout for the newfound boost

from the health advocates. "Science and faith had joined around a single topic," he said. "Not only was it good for you as a matter of faith, it was good for your body." While religion spoke of the transformative power of forgiveness for the whole world, those using the scientific methods were discovering how beneficial it was at the small end of the telescope, the individual. The health people had apparently "got it," and that was intriguing, especially for a film that sought to corroborate the power of forgiveness in every way possible.

The problem of finding a key to building a film was solved, Doblmeier said, when he hit upon the proposal by a group of New Yorkers to build a "Garden of Forgiveness" on a patch of ground at the site of the 9/11 attacks. The idea struck him as a focal point for the ultimate contradiction: attaching the word *forgiveness* to a place that symbolized ultimate evil, placing an olive branch in a vat of seething resentment. If it could be done there, even symbolically, perhaps it could be done anywhere.

Lyndon Harris, the Episcopal priest who had directed St. Paul's Chapel relief efforts at the World Trade Center location, was now head of the Sacred City Project, which hoped to win support for the garden. As he defined it in *The Power of Forgiveness*, the garden was envisioned as a place where "people can come and at least reflect on the possibility of forgiveness." It would in no way "excuse horrific acts by evil people" or "condone acts of terrorism." The purpose, he said, was "to invite people to decide intentionally to opt out of that cycle of violence and revenge." Harris's perspective was religious; another of the project sponsors, Fred Luskin of the Stanford University Forgiveness Project, took a more secular stance in favor of giving up personal hatreds.

Idyllic as it might have sounded to those attuned to such a garden, the concept was a hard sell to New Yorkers, many of whom were still smarting from the attacks. Some thought it sheer lunacy, evidence of the temptation to go "soft" on the enemy. Despite the claims by Harris and others that the garden was intended to bring about a healthier, saner climate, their appeals could barely be heard above the cries for revenge. Acknowledging the uphill fight, Harris noted the observation by biblical scholar Walter Wink, "that in our society, the only redemptive force we believe in really, if we look at everything, if we examine our culture, it seems to be, that we . . . believe in the myth of redemptive violence."

Lyndon Harris has proposed a "Garden of Forgiveness" at the site of the 9/11 attacks.

Doblmeier saw little "inclination to reconcile" or to insert the word *forgiveness* into this sacred 16-acre plot. Worthy as he believed the idea was, Doblmeier thought it was widely seen by self-appointed keepers of the disaster memory as a "foolhardy venture." This dimension of forgiveness involved a person's status as an American who was at the same time a citizen of the world. That required a way of thinking about such things as the cause of friction between the United States and other nations, dealing with the after-effects of terrorism and the responsibility of facing the possibilities of American wrongdoing. This kind of thinking didn't coincide exactly with a typical crisis in personal relations among people who knew each other. For obvious reasons, the bigger picture received less attention, but there was a strong link between the public and personal aspects of the forgiveness challenge. They invited similar reflexes of the heart.

Luskin made the connection in the Doblmeier film. His model can apply to persons and nations. "I can be hurt by you and decide that I have to make sure that you don't hurt me again. I can do it with hatred in my heart, or I can do it with some sense of compassion for my predicament, or I can do it with a sense of forgiving the human qualities that lead people to do harsh, violent acts. But I still want

Fred Luskin, of the Stanford Forgiveness Project, urged that considering forgiveness and ensuring security are not incompatible.

to make sure that I'm safe. And what we're suggesting through our garden is that you can reflect on ways to keep yourself safe without having to be hate-filled or as vengeance-minded as the people who did this to us."

The particular became the universal; the universal, the particular.

The garden proposal, and the debate it sparked, became the springboard for Doblmeier's quest for others who were qualified to address the issue scientifically and spiritually. He found Enright's research and his peace-making initiatives in Northern Ireland; Worthington's college teachings on the benefits of letting the anger go; the disarming visit of the Amish to forgive the killer of their children; the Buddhist master of compassion, Thich Nhat Hanh; the father of a boy who was murdered and the grandfather of the murderer; and a host of others who devoted their energies and talents to making forgiveness an appealing alternative.

INVITATION TO CHOOSE

At this point, with apologies to the experts, I don an amateur film critic's cap to offer a few opinions about the documentary's contents. The film moves seamlessly from one illustration to another, some of them large-scale settings, such as Ireland and 9/11. The social scientists make their case, effectively for the most part; and, while it's perhaps safe to assume that the public already knows much about the religious beliefs behind forgiveness, the reality is that few people know much. The science part pretty well explains its methods and guiding assumptions. The relevant teachings of major religions, primarily Christianity and Judaism, are sketched quickly and basically, enough to remind those familiar with these traditions but perhaps too little for those who may be undereducated in such matters. The shifting scenes focus on one-way street forgiveness, leaving the common two-way street variety more to the imagination. The essential questions about forgiveness—whether someone needs to ask for it, whether a confession is necessary, whether it is an absolute necessity, whether some offenses are beyond redemption—are embedded within the film at least implicitly. A two-way encounter would have been welcome but wasn't needed to carry out the film's purpose.

In its entirety, the documentary achieves something more significant than religious or scientific instruction; it invites viewers to choose for themselves the grand promise of forgiveness in a manner that lends the choice both urgency and appeal. Its poignancy is borne out by the people who lined up to speak to Doblmeier about the depths it touched in them. In his depictions of them and their stories, they responded not primarily on a thought level or an emotional level but from the core of themselves. It had rearranged—for the time being at least—the furniture in their existential living rooms.

Though much of the documentary touches on world problems, Doblmeier found little interest among those attending previews in the wider issues of reconciliation. The after-movie sessions dwelt almost exclusively on the trials among people who knew each other well and had become separated by the actions of one or more of them. Often nobody had tried to get back together; mutual alienation had settled in, sometimes for decades. Either it was a logjam that no one wanted to dislodge for fear of further damage or an emotional morass whose origins had been long lost. But the strife was, psychically speaking, local, and Doblmeier's rounds rarely focused on a nation wracked by hostilities or a seemingly intractable problem, such as the hatred between Palestinians and Israelis. And understandably so. With certain exceptions, such as South Africa, where progress has lifted spirits, most examples of ethnic or political strife and hatred exhibit so little hope as to discourage efforts toward forgiveness by persons struggling with the resentments among those nearest to them.

The typical post-preview candidate was someone reminded of a painful break with a relative or friend. The fracture had been brought about by something that had shattered trust, the one indispensable element in close human bonding. The trust was gone, and it took an act of daring by one or the other or both to restore it to one degree or another. The potential for further hurt often prevented taking that risk. Things froze.

One evening a woman spoke to Doblmeier, the pastor apparent, about her sister. Events had driven them apart, and they had remained apart for many years. Then came word that her sister was dying. She made contact and, in her words, "we solved the issues the best we could." She was "proud to say it," she told Doblmeier, adding, "I got myself straight."

Death, of course, was for many the final prompter. I am reminded of that beautiful odyssey of a movie, *The Straight Story*, based on a true account of 73-year-old Alvin Straight, who crept across the state of Iowa on a lawnmower (he'd lost his driver's license when he could no longer drive a car) after he heard that his brother had been felled by a stroke. The pair hadn't spoken forever, but word of the brother's plight sent Alvin packing, or puttering, as it were. He reached his brother in Wisconsin in time, and the two old bulls made amends in that ancient, male, wordless way.

Everyone, it seemed, had a deathbed forgiveness story that tended toward the bittersweet. The break in the dam of antagonism was welcome, often tearful, but the underside was the nagging question of why it took so long and had to go to such extremes. Two old goats (or two young kids for that matter) remain at loggerheads long after the origin of the dispute has faded from memory until some emergency pops the lid and mercy flows.

Frequently the ending is not so happy, as the filmmaker experienced recently within his own family. His wife, Jelena Vucetic, was raised in Belgrade, Serbia, in a family that included two uncles she treasured. The brothers had long been companions and the best of friends. Then came the day that words drove them apart. The blow took the form of the older brother belittling of the younger man's pruning of trees in the back yard. They walled off from one another, resisting the efforts of Doblmeier's wife to bring them back together. Not long ago, a phone call informed the Doblmeiers that the older brother

had died. His niece hastened to ask if her two cherished uncles had repaired the damage between them before the end. They had not.

Doblmeier's personal views on forgiveness are available for the asking. While he might wince at being called an evangelist of forgiveness, he has clearly become an emissary for it. He is a messenger who carries the message. To make the film, he became a student of the phenomenon and wound up a convinced practitioner.

His understanding of forgiveness had evolved over the years. Having grown up in a German-Irish Catholic family in Queens, New York, he was introduced to confession along with his peers and, like many initiates to the sacrament, paid rather perfunctory attention to it during his school years, neither dismissing nor embracing it. Before undertaking the film, he said he thought of forgiveness as a "spare tire" that was available if he needed it in a pinch. It was nothing difficult; an easy ace in the hole. He vaguely knew the Bible recommended it and Jesus acted on it. But it wasn't anything urgent or taxing.

The process of making the documentary turned his assumptions upside down. He uses Enright's idea of "forgiveness glasses" to emphasize how radically his perspective changed. To help children in Northern Ireland overcome bad feelings toward one another, Enright had them wear simple sunglasses to emphasize the possibility of looking at the same thing differently. Doblmeier applied that exercise as a metaphor for his turnabout. "I was forced to put on forgiveness glasses in order to see the central paradigm of forgiveness—the ability to let the anger and resentment go," he said.

What he also saw through these symbolic spectacles was that forgiveness wasn't optional but a full-fledged commandment on a par with the ones that told Christians to worship the true God and to skip adultery. Forgiving, Doblmeier suddenly acknowledged, was central rather than peripheral to the life of believers because Jesus had intended it as a required part of the life exam rather than an item of extra credit. That is, Jesus wasn't kidding. He expected, as Doblmeier stated it, to put "into action the fundamental commandment of the New Testament to love one another."

FORGIVENESS AND THE AMERICAN ETHOS

Doblmeier sallied forth to the showings of his documentary with hopes that were tempered by what he perceived as harsh realities. Jesus might have instructed his followers to give up their resentments and to confess their own

offenses, but those sentiments didn't sell well in a society that prized a stiff-upper-lip mentality and derision for "losers." American society made it tough to admit mistakes, let alone grave sins, suffused as it was by a competitive ethic that placed a premium on hiding what might be considered "weaknesses." As years of big business scandals had demonstrated, corporate America wasn't wallowing in an ethic of altruistic forgiveness. Self-help forgiveness, maybe, as a means of bolstering employee health, but that was about the extent of it, if even that. The nation's credo, after all, was self-gain, honoring anything that helped achieve that end. Forgiveness itself had gained a new franchise on the basis of its ability to improve one's vital signs.

The drive toward personal success was rightly defended as an incentive to develop one's talents and to allow cream to rise to the top. Competition was the legitimate vehicle for that purpose. The problem, so far as the forgiveness factor was concerned, was that concern for the common good, which could offset some of the severe results of radical individualism, was fast fading. Public acceptance of that kind of counter-weight had diminished. Concepts like self-sacrifice and social welfare became more peripheral to everyday thought. The idea that forgiveness might benefit the community as a whole was regarded as strange. Though we had good insights into how education for the poorest children could be achieved, for example, we weren't about to provide the resources to do it. That was "their" problem, one that, by coincidence or not, guaranteed a steady supply of minimum-wage workers for private enterprise. Likewise, we could include everyone in health care, but we choose instead to keep it as a privilege of the "deserving" who can afford it.

That wasn't a landscape very hospitable to self-denial and the "new commandment" that Doblmeier had identified, but there was an opening for the subject that his film appealed to. The theme of the film ran against the country's pragmatic grain, but it hadn't been totally run out of the public mind. Though the path of forgiveness might be countercultural in the sense that it struck many as incompatible with the American way of life—quaint, even romantic, but impractical—its appeal to some might just lie in its foreignness.

The American ethos might balk at forgiveness as the behavior of a "softie" (the fear of "giving in to the person who hurt them"). But there was, Doblmeier believed, a remnant on the memory track of many people that prodded them to think they "should" forgive and somehow were expected to. That was at least a start. His after-showing talks with viewers reinforced his view that the gap between the commandment and the performance of it was yawning indeed. "Doing it was what was hard," he said, even though it had been deeply ingrained. "Many people I spoke with felt a lot of angst," he recalled. They wondered, "What do I do?" They were struggling.

ANGUISH AND PARALYSIS

It was immediately apparent to Doblmeier that the film's tale of various people wrestling with forgiveness in various settings had touched that deep nerve. It was connected to anguish and paralysis, the imperative to do something in response to the rage that was tearing them up inside, the commandment of the Lord, and the circumstances of their lives bottled up by fear of letting go and appearing weak.

The fight to overcome the barriers became a major topic among those who lined up to speak to the filmmaker. It resembled an evangelist's altar call, except that Doblmeier wasn't appearing as an evangelist and not everybody was ready to be saved. Perhaps it was more accurate to see it as the altar call before the altar call to distinguish between the sister who had made amends with her dying sister and the brother of the Korean War casualty who remained inconsolable.

For Doblmeier, the "power" of forgiveness was never in doubt. If anything, it had taken on "elevated importance as a central message of the Gospel." As he listened, moreover, he grew more convinced that there was no such thing as what he called "cheap forgiveness" (after Bonhoeffer's concept of "cheap grace," which he defined as an attempt to win God's favor and forgiveness by going through superficial motions). Only an honest and sincere heart was capable of attaining it, he said; otherwise, it just doesn't work, leaving the person holding on to the anger, consciously or not. The test of whether the seeker was authentic, he said, was if a person "no longer felt angry about the hurt when re-visiting it and yet not forgetting it." The ability to imagine working through the difficulty in peace, while not forgetting it, was a sign that the transformation had taken place.

Nothing was more crucial yet more difficult than making forgiveness a reality among those whom you loved and with whom you lived, he thought. But whether the source of injury was oneself, a loved one, or a stranger, the standard of behavior remained the same. "I need to remember that the person who has hurt me is also a child of God," he said quietly. "That takes a lot out of a need to retaliate. Seeing the face of God takes away much of the anger. The need to forgive touches the deepest human expectations; it calls forth the divine within us."

He undertook the film in large measure because the scope of forgiveness' power had broadened with the emergence of the scientific studies of its benefits. "Faith communities have preached it for thousands of years," he said. "Now it has given rise to investigation by scientists. They are finding a way to approach this together—it's a wonderful intersection at the start of the twenty-first century." While the forgiveness scholars seemed to aim more at a narrower self-improvement target than religion with its tradition of blessing the other, Doblmeier cautioned against a sharp separation of the two. The picture was much more mixed, he believed. Altruists, religious or otherwise, generally included themselves as beneficiaries in the good will they exhibited; likewise, many self-helpers saw the benefits to themselves as a prelude to being of service to others. One example of this complexity grew out of his talks with audience members. Many people said they'd felt that if they'd paid sufficient attention to self-forgiveness they wouldn't have done the bad things that produced even bigger problems.

THE ONGOING CHALLENGE OF UNFORGIVENESS

Obviously, most people left the showings of film without having passed along a personal review to Doblmeier. Those who did likely sought him out because they felt an urgent need to tell him something or had been moved deeply during the showing. One of Doblmeier's observations about the audiences was that they came expecting the film to show "the unforgiveness issues they faced in their own lives." There were always those who wondered why certain things were not included. Like so many in the gatherings, they often impressed him as "hurting through no fault of their own by abuse or betrayal." This sampling wasn't representative by any scientific standards, yet it was a peek at the underside of the rock of relative silence about such matters. It showed something vital about the depths of suffering that existed to a greater or lesser extent throughout the greater population. Message: there's a lot of concealed pain out there that is related to forgiveness.

Further evidence came from those who responded to Journey Films's invitation to forward their reactions on an Internet site. The survey included three open-ended queries: (1) Was there someone they were now thinking of forgiving? (2) How did they see their thoughts about forgiveness changing? (3) What might they take to put those changes into action? Hundreds of viewers submitted answers that provided a revealing scattering of thoughts and feelings.

The tenor of these responses is generally tentative and often plaintive. The things people have to say about themselves after seeing the film are disarming and modest. They have crept into the subject like Sandberg's "little cat feet," antenna up and caution flags at half-mast. It signals a willingness to "begin" rather than a claim to have arrived.

"I might realize that it isn't an act of weakness to forgive, but that it is a strength," says one. Another awakened to the possibility that forgiveness was "a bridge between a God of justice and a God of love." Humans were "hardwired for justice and revenge. Forgiveness is a miracle, a way we heal."

One viewer vowed not only to "be more open to the idea" but to "think of it sooner rather than later. It's something that comes slowly. I need to begin the habit of forgiveness." Said another: "I see it more for me than for the other person, but I don't know how to go about it. How do you really forgive someone?"

Cutting to the chase with touching honesty, another simply expressed astonishment over "the fact that I'm thinking about it at all."

For some, a person to forgive or to be forgiven by came promptly to mind. "Tracy." "I may call up my ex-boyfriend to see how he's doing." "I need to ask the Lord to help me overcome my anger for my ex-wife." "Christa."

Gaining compassion was a major theme. "I'd do better if I forgave myself first," said one. "I plan to be more compassionate and forgiving if people are not honest with me and when people don't act as I expect when it comes to honesty." Sometimes the film delivered a humble reminder of fallibility: "I have a sincere desire to forgive [my stepmother] and most times I feel I have. Now and then, my anger resurfaces and I work on forgiveness again. I do not feel I was insincere when I forgave her before, nor do I feel I failed at forgiveness. I wake up each day and pray for a forgiving heart. It opens my heart to love her as a child of God."

"Pride keeps me from it," said one filmgoer who pledged to "try harder to accept people as they are not the way I want them to be." A related account: "the ripple effect makes swallowing my pride and accepting the past unpleasantness very worthwhile attempting."

Other beginnings: "I can see it is okay to still hold on to the memory but let the anger and bad feelings go." "I believe I will be much more open to forgiving myself and others now and more aware of the benefits of forgiving." "I have recently begun to see forgiveness as a way that we human beings can set ourselves free; in that sense it is really ultimately a gift we give ourselves." "The response of the Amish to the shootings was an incredibly powerful message for me, and it was then I really began to think about forgiveness as a real tool for change."

The Amish sequence factored into another kind of reaction. One viewer was still ambivalent about the value of forgiveness but was now inclined to think the Amish had it right: "It may be something you 'do' first and work to 'feel' second." Echoing that sentiment, said another: "I don't think I need to change the way I think, but about the way I actually do or do not forgive. It's easier said than done."

Especially when it came to the two-way street dilemmas. A son had a grudge against his parents that the parents, who were reporting this situation, felt was unfair. Nonetheless, they said they'd asked his forgiveness and he'd refused. Now, they said, "we want to forgive him for not forgiving us." Or: "I am still working on a hurt that happened twenty years ago. I finally came to accept my role in allowing the behavior that hurt me. I no longer wish to retaliate, but am not quite to the full grace of forgiving the person."

The sound mind, sound body claims also drew interest. "I didn't know about the health benefits." "I see even more than previously how good, beneficial, healthy it is to forgive another."

Sprinkled among the responses were the kindly sermonettes. "I realize that though there are incidents I may not forget, I can forgive people. Everyone deserves a chance and forgiveness. We are God's children and as God's children we are called to forgive others as they would forgive us. I have found it more peaceful to forgive and am starting to love my enemies because they need love."

A few made it clear that their thinking hadn't shifted one iota. One added the warning that pressuring people into forgiveness before they've genuinely let go of anger can cause more harm than good.

As the house lights rise, the question remains: to forgive or not to forgive. Within the framework of most discussions, this is more an answer than a question. The assumption within religious traditions and increasingly among social scientists is that you'd be crazy not to. In forgiveness lies the means of salvation and improved mental and cardiovascular health. Who in his or her right mind would deliberately choose not to forgive when those gifts are readily available? The "answer," therefore, is to get with forgiveness. The "question" is whether you will do it.

Another assumption is that forgiveness is the only solution to the problem of clogged up resentment toward others and murderous schemes of revenge, and at least part of the solution to depression and hypertension. While such a conclusion is well justified by spiritual and moral teachings and many psychological studies, it doesn't cover all the means by which human beings appear to cope with anger and vengeful feelings. On the surface, at least, some people seem to live reasonably normal lives without forgiving others or asking to be pardoned for miserable things they've done to others. Perhaps one's approach to these matters is determined largely by upbringing and individual sensibilities. Genetics may tell us someday that some people are more prone to seek the forgiveness answer than others. Repression and denial are thought to be generally harmful (though Sigmund Freud thought civilization was made possible by them), but they have long been mechanisms for staving off the hunger for forgiveness. Nothing about this devalues the worth of forgiveness. It only suggests that it may not be a universal imperative.

It's just a hunch, but I suspect most people die with at least a few unforgiveness arrows in their moral quivers. The point is whether we should try to divest ourselves of as many of them as possible before we meet that end.

The case for forgiveness based on the spiritual-scientific findings is compelling. In deciding which way to go, we have raised several key concerns that can act as guides.

First, do you consider forgiveness a strength or a weakness? Most societies, certainly America, regard it as soft; so if you choose to go ahead, be conscious that it is a rather counter-cultural thing to do. Maybe that's a good reason to do it. Forgiveness is the road not taken; but, as many wise people have reminded us over the centuries, the conventional road runs smack into a brick wall.

Second, why would you want to do it? Maybe you believe it will help restore you to sanity or fortify your immune system. In other words, you see personal dividends. Or perhaps your faith tells you that Jesus or Allah or Yahweh or Buddha orders you to, or something to that effect. That is to say, your forgiving would contribute somehow to the fulfillment of the divine creation. You may be looking for rewards for yourself or looking for cosmic redemption. Some, without apology, want something better for themselves. Others are more altruistic. Motives make a difference. On the other hand, maybe you just cannot do it—and there may be good reasons not to.

Third, what would you require to transact forgiveness? Does another person have to ask you for it? Do you need recompense? Do you ask nothing of the sort, granting it because a higher power has told you to? What kind of criteria would you set down? Is it enough to know that you'll be better off by doing it, or can't you envision being better off unless guilty ones pay some kind of price? If you're the guilty one, or if both you and the other are guilty, what standards would work there? Are you prepared to let go of anger—and have an idea what that means? Or do you still need more time to be angry? Forgiveness entails risk. Maybe you won't get what you want. Maybe you'll have to keep forgiving the same thing. Can you take that step into uncertainty? Are you ready to love your neighbor—actually?

Finally, have you thought about where the power of forgiveness comes from? Is it generated within the psyche of the human being? Does it derive from an essence of the divine within everyone, known as the soul? Is it a mind game used to rid ourselves of haunting thoughts? How we define that source may not be decisive because it's possible to tap into strengths and powers within ourselves of which we are not always conscious, but it does help guide our direction in seeking forgiveness.

Forgiveness has been elevated as "divine" while erring is labeled "human." A rising chorus of witnesses propose that forgiveness might become more human for the sake of a better world.

Index of Persons

Index of Subjects

Filmmaker's Acknowledgments

We at Journey Films are delighted with publication of this volume, companion to our film *The Power of Forgiveness*. With this book, readers will be able to explore the whole reality of forgiveness in its personal, social, and even global dimensions. Our thanks to Kenneth Briggs for an inspired text, and to Fortress Press for its confidence in the project.

Birthing a film, like building a city, is best accomplished as the work of many skilled hands. In the case of *The Power of Forgiveness*, the credit list is long, but two people in particular immeasurably shaped the film's final character and form. Dan Juday and Adele Schmidt—both producers for the film—brought creativity and imagination to the daily process and made the whole experience of crafting the film nothing less than a joy. They also provided assistance, both creative and practical, in the forging of this book.

Tim Finkbiner was the film's on-line or finishing editor, and as the last person to handle the film his masterful touch proved all the more critical.

The Power of Forgiveness film (and by extension, the book) was only possible because of the support of two foundations committed to fostering a deeper understanding of forgiveness —The John Templeton Foundation and Fetzer Institute. In particular, we thank Pamela Thompson, Andrew Rick-Miller, and Mickey Olivanti for their continued faith in our work. Thanks, too, goes to Polly Kosko and Bobbi Kennedy from South Carolina public television.

Finally, thanks to my wife, Jelena, and son, Nik, who make all things special. Over the years I've too often tested their gift of forgiveness.

Martin Doblmeier
Journeyfilms.com

Additional Acknowledgments

The author, publisher, and filmmaker are happy to acknowledge support of the Fetzer Institute and its Campaign for Love & Forgiveness in the promotion of this volume. The Fetzer Institute's mission, to foster awareness of the power of love and forgiveness in the emerging global community, rests on the conviction that efforts to address the critical issues facing the world must go beyond political, social, and economic strategies to their psychological and spiritual roots. Its work is grounded in a conviction that the relationship between our inner lives of mind and spirit and our outer lives of action and service holds the key to lasting change. The institute is not a religious organization. But it operates on a belief that profound change comes from deep spiritual understanding of what guides human beliefs and behaviors—we learn from all wisdom traditions. For further materials related to this book, visit the Fetzer Institute at http://www.fetzerinstitute.org.